Wallsend Best

A Personal Experience of the Rising Sun Colliery Wallsend, 1941-67

by Ron Curran

This book is dedicated to my dad, John Ross Curran, a miner of the old school, born 1876 in Annbank, Ayrshire, Scotland. He was a trapper boy at the age of nine to fourteen working in Annbank Colliery, Ayrshire and a coal hewer at Dixon's Colliery, Lanarkshire. He later worked at Hazelrigg and Dinnington in Northumberland, and lastly was a checkweighman at the Rising Sun Colliery, Northumberland.

He was a soldier in the Boer War (1899-02), fought in the First World War (1914-18), in Dad's Army, the Home Guard, (1939-45). He died in 1960 at the age of 83 years. He served his country and the miners well.

'Lang may your lum reek' he would often say as an admirer of Rabbie Burns, meaning 'long may your fire burn'. A very appropriate saying for a miner. I couldn't have said it better. And I am proud to say that his son Ian, my elder brother, played a lament 'Flowers of the Forest' on my dad's bagpipes at the pit-head on the day that the Rising Sun finally set.

Previous page: A postcard titled 'The New Colliery, Wallsend' from around 1910.

This book is a revised edition, originally published in 2008.

Copyright Ron Curran 2009

First published in 2009 by

Summerhill Books
PO Box 1210
Newcastle-upon-Tyne
NE99 4AH

Email: andrew_clark@hotmail.co.uk

ISBN: 978-1-906721-13-8

No part of this publication may be reproduced, stored in a mechanical retrieval system, or transmitted, in any form or by any means, electronic, mechanical, photocopying, recording or otherwise, without prior permission of the author.

Contents

Acknowledgements	4
Introduction	7
1. Wallsend Best	12
2. The Wallsend and Hebburn Coal Company	16
3. Pit Ponies	32
4. Early Days and Early Times	40
5. Nationalisation – They Are Our Pits Now!	52
6. Welfare	69
7. Mining Memories	76
8. Fighting to Save the Pit	97
9. The Sun Sets For Good	109

Acknowledgements

I have been overwhelmed and delighted at the response to my appeal for photographs and stories relating to the Rising Sun Colliery, Wallsend. I almost immediately received telephone calls, emails and letters from sons, daughters, mothers, brothers and sisters and from some of the miners and mechanics themselves who spent some part of their life at the Rising Sun. And almost all of them said the comradeship in sharing dangers, sometimes hardship and facing mutual problems created a common bond which has lasted beyond the life of the pit. There was something special in that relationship and it reached beyond the enclosures of the pit, out into homes, the allotments, the pubs and clubs, where the bonhomie of the pitmen was always apparent. Their language was called 'pitmatic' and full of witticisms and good humour, with a bit less of the strong language of the coal face.

The trigger for writing this book was receiving a newspaper cutting from a friend, of the blacksmiths of the Rising Sun posing on Vesting Day (First day of Nationalisation) in 1947 outside the blacksmith's shop at the colliery. The chargeman blacksmith Tommy Hughes, who was also cagesmith and branch secretary of the mechanics at the time, hoisted the NCB flag on the flagpole of No. 2 shaft. The memories keep flooding back and despite having had a successful career as a full time union official for 23 years, my heart remained with my mates at the pit and our neighbours in Wallsend.

I received a letter from Leslie (Les) Francis, the only blacksmith still living who was an apprentice in the blacksmiths' shop when I started in 1942. I welcome and value his letter because he is the only person who could verify in total, everything that happened while I was there in the blacksmiths' shop. His letter is printed in full:

'Dear Ron, I have been looking at the work you are doing in our local newspaper. I always said that you were too good for blacksmithing when you used to sketch the lads faces in the blacksmith's shop on a piece of writing paper. Well now, I hear you are taking on a big job writing a book about the Rising Sun Colliery. I thought you would have tackled that job earlier as a lot of the real miners that worked there will be dead. But never mind Ron, I know you will be successful in your venture. I don't know what happened to all our old mates. I know just a few have passed on but I don't know about the others. Well Ron, I will close now wishing you and your family all the best, Les'. That really is a voice from the past. I telephoned him and had not heard his voice since 1967, over 40 years ago.

Also I must make special mention to Veronica Swinney who visited North Tyneside libraries, first Wallsend and then North Shields for any information they may hold about the Rising Sun Colliery. She found a virtual goldmine and then telephoned me suggesting I go down personally. Veronica's dad, Jack (Pedlar) Palmer, and grandfather

Richard Palmer both worked at the Rising Sun and both raced whippets there. Thank you Veronica!

However, I must make one more special mention. Jim Lucas (usually called Harry at the pit), former ventilation officer sent me the first photograph which immediately struck me as a must for the book's cover. It is of the last four men, each one named, coming out of the pit for the very last time. And also for giving me the closing dates of the last man riding day, of the ventilation, and capping of Nos 1 and 2 shafts.

Author Ron Curran with Steve and David Allerdyce – the two sons of Alex, my best friend at the pit.

Almost without exception, mention is made by contributors to the 'best time of our lives' or words to that affect. But I think the one that encapsulates the feeling more completely is in an email from Lorraine who said, 'Sitting here writing this to you has took me on an 'all our yesterdays' trip down memory lane'. She was writing about her dad, Big Joe Stoddart, as she calls him. He was an overman at the pit.

I have also received messages from the nephew of Jack Thompson former colliery manager, the son of colliery engineer Jack Hamil and other people in management. That is of course, apart from the many underground miners and surface workers and craftsmen who remember with affection, or sometimes sorrow, some of the incidents or accidents that occurred in their own personal experience. I find it amazing the number of children of the miners who have written with warmth about their memories, and sometimes even their grandchildren.

Left: *Ron and Doreen Curran with Mrs Dodds, grandmother to Shirley Grice (née Sansom). Shirley was a small girl when we were neighbours in Laurel Street, Wallsend. Shirley's father was a blacksmith at 'The Sun'. Later in the book Shirley shares her memories of being Band Major in the Rising Sun Colliery Legionnaires Juvenile Jazz Band.*

Let me also thank the *Newcastle Journal* for publishing my letter appealing for information in the first instance followed by the *Evening Chronicle* article with the full story. I am most grateful to them both as well as journalist Nigel Green; and the *News Guardian*.

To my wife Doreen for her patience and help in receiving telephone calls, writing the information given, and being even more patient during my absences to North Shields Library and Wallsend Library, and elsewhere. Without whom I could not have completed this book.

I am keeping to last the wonderful people who said they would do everything possible to help, including sending some wonderful photographs and memorabilia. There are too many to name in person but their generosity and kindness is beyond belief and I sincerely hope the book justifies their expectations.

Left: *Doreen my wife was always a winner. She got me didn't she? This was taken at the sports field at 'The Sun' about the mid 1950s. There were two memorable events that I remember that day. The first was when Doreen beat me hands down on the shooting gallery. The other was when a young boy about fourteen joined in the fun at putting the shot. To the amazement of all the blacksmiths (about six) waiting to show their skill and strength. He threw this heavy metal ball at least six feet further than anybody else. What a disgrace!*

Picture Credits

The publisher would like to thank the following who have supplied photographs for the book:

Derek Gillum, Mike Kirkup, Evan Martin, George Nairn, Billy Ward.

Many thanks to photographer Rob McGinley for his pictures on pages 114 and 115.

Introduction

This story is about a journey through 25 years of my life at the Rising Sun Colliery, Wallsend-on-Tyne from 1942 to 1967. During that time I witnessed incidents that I know I will never see again, such as a tiny piebald pit pony called Pride having a ride in the blackness of the pit on a rubber conveyor belt from inbye (the coalface) to the stables, and quite capable of finding its own way. Of a cat (domiciled in the stable to keep the mice down) having a field day when the ponies arrived from inbye at their stable and throwing out through the air with their lips the unfortunate little mice. Thereafter the cat was like an international goalkeeper until it tired of the game. Of seeing a blacksmith during his 'bait time' pull a violin out a box and begin playing classical music in the blacksmith's shop. Of standing beside a belt driven drop hammer and witnessing a young blacksmith have two fingers flattened. Or watching blacksmith Old Fin frying cabbage on his fire along with eggs and bacon as a starter before he ate his cow pie which he heated in the labourers' cabin. And remembering the sobering sight of seeing a stretcher being carried to the medical centre following death due to a fall of stone underground. I myself nearly witnessed or was part of an accident from a roof fall underground where we always sat for a breather while the horseshoer and I were in the Low Main Seam stables shoeing a pony and, unaccountably, the horseshoer changing his mind at the last minute. And lastly, but by no means least, meeting characters at the pit who in terms of eccentricity would take some beating.

Inevitably, the environment in which we worked and the whole shared atmosphere, especially underground of potential danger, linked us all into a social bond that blossomed into social activities such as the creation of a pit football team, a whippet club, the miners' Annual Leek Show, the Annual Christmas Treat for pensioners and their wives, and other events such as miners' Jolly Boys. These were entertainers with a difference, all of which allowed the harsh reality of work to recede for a while at least and see each other in a different light. The centre of these activities was the Miners' Welfare Hall, an important meeting place for the community spirit that it engendered. This was revealed especially with the establishment of the Juvenile Jazz Band, fetching the children into the fold.

The men from the last cage up at the Rising Sun Colliery, Wallsend, on 18th July 1969.

The tapestry of history, even local history, is often intangible in the making but its thread of gold is its continuity through many scores of years of hardship, personal suffering, sometimes grief and always neighbourliness. That bond prevailed from the pit face to the pit houses, the backyards and sometimes the picket lines. Coalmining was not just a job, it was a livelihood and when that is threatened the bond is at its strongest. Perhaps it is not widely known that the Welfare contributed through deductions of 3p per week per man (3d old money which was much more than new pence) to the Tynemouth Royal Jubilee Infirmary and also deductions towards the Miners' Homes for retired miners. I know that because my dad, Jock Curran, Checkweighman at the colliery, was a governor on both bodies.

Nor can I ignore the economic issue which after all is the bread and butter of all our lives. That is why I try to show in this book as a strong thread, the fight for the life of the Rising Sun pit, even sometimes meeting opposition from some surprising quarters. You may be reading for the very first time the whole story about this, and because there will now be few around us today to confirm or deny what I say, I have to rely upon the local newspapers of the day to back up my story.

Nor does the Labour Government of Harold Wilson come out in a good light. Promises were made and not kept, and the evidence of the reason to close the pits become clear only in the course of time. The book ends sadly but appropriately with the blowing up of the concrete and glass tower of No. 3 shaft, sunk as a long-term lifesaver for the Rising Sun and mining in the area as a whole.

I try to give the answer why it died. When a Tory Government eventually destroyed what remained a still quite sizable part of the mining industry they were just finishing the job that Harold Wilson and his Labour Government began, although not with the same cold, calculated, and callous brutality of the Tories. Never did I think I would ever have to say this as a Labour Party certificated member of over fifty years. But my heart belongs to the mining fraternity, and only my time and effort is given on loan to those who say they support a cause that I believe in. If however they betray that cause they betray everything I stand for. And the cause that I believe in is the fraternity of communities, where social awareness is bred and fostered, where honesty is a basic precept and integrity is a virtue. It is within this communal spirit that neighbourliness is an accepted responsibility without an expected reward, where the elderly are respected

The Rising Sun Lodge Banner at the Miners' Picnic.

and the children cherished and where the value of worth is measured in people's actions and not money. That is the worth of the mining communities in this country, and for that, they and their children are the salt of the earth.

Lastly, to those who believe that the demise of the mining industry was inevitable, let me say that in 1960 we had a viable coal industry with vast reserves under the soil of the British Isles. We had also discovered oil and gas under the sea around our shores to the envy of many countries in the Western World. Gas and electricity were publicly owned and we again had a Labour Government. However, rather than planning how best to use these joint resources to our best advantage, gas, electricity and coal were encouraged to compete against each other in separate fuel markets, even though gas and electricity were fuel buyers and coal a fuel producer. The demands for a planned integrated fuel policy was therefore ignored and worse still, the wolves of the oil industry were invited into the North Sea and hey presto! Bit-by-bit our great Christmas Box of North Sea oil became almost a free-for-all. The fall guy in all of this furore was king coal, seen as the only British competitor likely to stand up against these international invaders.

If this all sounds rather theatrical, nevertheless, that is the reality, coal was thrown to the wolves. If we haven't been betrayed we were certainly deserted, by a Labour Government. My last words on this is that it was in communities such as the miners, dockers, shipyard workers, iron and steel workers, seamen, agricultural workers and labourers that the Labour Party was born during the turmoil of the Industrial Revolution. And it is that history that the Labour Party should always remember. Political parties who have the power for change, are like people, not remembered by the coats they wear but what they do and where they came from.

Right: *The Rising Sun Target Board – a huge target board set up in the yard where everybody could see what was expected of them. Targets were set in an office environment, light years away from the coal face where the hazards and problems exist.*

My family

My mother, a native of Wallsend (born in 1896), was visiting her father's birthplace in Huddersfield when she was young. As she stepped off the train a large hoarding said "Buy Wallsend Best Coal". She said she was thrilled to bits that Wallsend had followed her to Huddersfield. This was the first time I had ever heard the expression 'Wallsend Best' long before I started work at the pit. My mother told me that my dad was a checkweighman at the Rising Sun Colliery in Wallsend. Naturally she had to explain as well as she could the nature of his job. She made it simple. "He is paid by the men to see that the coal owner doesn't rob them of coal they have cut out of the coal face". I learned after I started at the pit that the checkweighman surveys the measurements of the weighman who is employed by the coal owner. If there is a discrepancy it goes to arbitration. Because of disputes over this, a Coal Mines' Act was introduced called the Truck Act which allowed, among other regulations, the checkweighman through law to carry out his job without harassment or victimisation from the coal owner or his managers.

However, much more significantly, I was informed fairly recently while visiting Scotland by the former general secretary of the Scottish Miners' Union, Eric Clarke MP, that it was common to employ a checkweighman from men who had been blacked by the employer following a strike. A black list of names of those miners who were known as union activists was sent around the coalfield to other coal owners for the purpose of banishing them and their families from the coalfield. This meant of course losing their homes also. Checkweighmen were generally selected from these blacked miners on the basis of their loyalty to the men and the union in past disputes. This therefore brings my own family into focus. According to my dad, his father Frank Curran was a miner and union activist in both Ayrshire and Lanarkshire, Scotland, and he was a supporter of Keir Hardie who at that time was agent for the Ayrshire Miners' Union. Dad started work as a trapper boy at the age of nine, in an Ayrshire coal mine being carried on his dad's back to the pit. My dad also told me, and I have no reason to doubt this, that his dad started work underground at the age of seven. Dad eventually became a coal hewer in pits in Lanarkshire, was blacked with the rest of the family after a great strike in 1894, and dad came down to Tyneside, first to Hazelrigg and then Dinnington collieries and then to Wallsend, again working as a coal hewer.

He started work at the Rising Sun Colliery before the General Strike of 1926. I have tried to be as accurate as possible with names and dates of a period now so long ago. I feel that this is essential to give authenticity to the story. For example, when I started at the Rising Sun Colliery, it was in the latter days of 1942. This would mean sometime between October and December 1942. I know this because it was blackout in the early morning on the first day I started shortly before the Christmas and New Year holiday. I would then be 15 years and about six months old and my following birthday would be in June at 16 years old when my actual apprenticeship would start. I left in June 1967 which from starting to finish was an exact period of 24 years and about nine months. Let me call it 25 years.

At the age of 80 years I have now lived a working life that has been in effect two different lives. The first was my (almost) 25 years at the Rising Sun Colliery which I now look upon as my formative years as a union official. It was also a time and a place that was rich with characters and full of incidents big and small that could never be matched in my later career as a full time officer, working in a large office full of secretaries and driving a union car around the West Riding of Yorkshire, then North Riding, Northumberland and Durham and more latterly Scotland and Northern Ireland. I look back upon my time at the Rising Sun as more variable, colourful and exciting than anything that has ever happened since although let me hasten to add that becoming president of the Scottish TUC in 1987 was the proudest moment of my life. But that is part of my second working life, in a different environment and no matter how interesting or even important, it cannot match living at the sharp end and facing the threat of the sack from time to time throughout a period from becoming a branch secretary at the age of 21 years to finally leaving the pit in June 1967. In total I have been a union official, both lay and full-time for a period of 42 years from 1948 to 1990, a contribution of which I am proud. In the first, I served the mining community as a lay official and in the second, a full time official for low paid workers in local government, universities and the health service. What they all had in common was respect from the public at large for the work they did and the contribution they made to people's lives. If only governments could have recognised and honoured that, few of the disputes would ever have taken place.

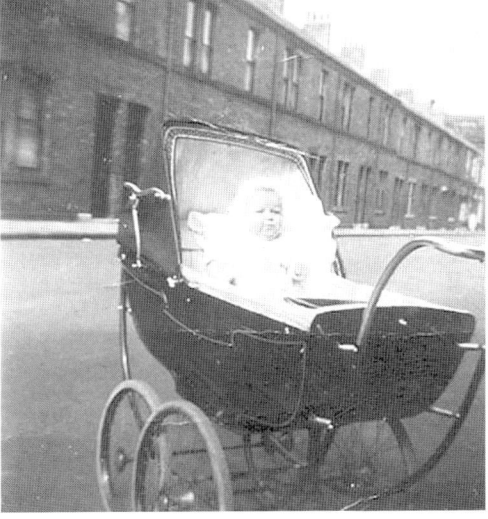

Right: *This picture shows our first born, Susan Curran aged about eight months in a pram in Laurel Street, Wallsend. The colliery houses were on the near side of the road (where the pram and our house is). This picture was taken in 1955. It was in this street that we grew to understand the spirit of the mining community of Wallsend and where our children grew up and went to school. It was also here where there was an 'open door' philosophy among neighbours, now I believe a thing of the past.*

Chapter 1
Wallsend Best

The following four articles give a brief account of 'Wallsend Best'.

Industrial Paradox of Tyneside
Story by Don Nicholl, *Weekly Chronicle*, 26th February 1949

'Around about the year 60 BC, there lived on the north bank of the River Tyne a fierce tribe of Britons known as the Ottodini – distinguished by their long red hair. Today, the land they tilled is carpeted with the dark houses of Wallsend and into the soil on which they raised their cattle, knives the deepest pit shaft in Northumberland. The shaft belongs to the Rising Sun Colliery, where manager John Thompson describes his miners as 'cosmopolitan'. By this he means that more of his men come from surrounding towns on Tyneside rather than Wallsend itself. This is an unusual feature for a town where industrial history is woven so strongly with its coal seams, yet it is true of many industrial concerns in Wallsend. For this is a town that is a paradox ... although it possesses strong native industries much of its working population is but a daily influx from Newcastle, Gosforth and the coast towns, and many full time inhabitants find their work outside the borough. This is a feature that has both advantages and disadvantages for, to quote Mr Thompson again on his miners, "In a small coalmining village you find the men live their work, even when they are actually not at work for they just can't get away from it. On the other hand, the men from outside leave their work behind them after their shift is done and pursue outside interests" ... a factor that needs money if only to provide the cash. Well whatever the reason they certainly do work hard in Wallsend.'

Men from the Rising Sun Colliery, with No. 1 shaft behind, in 1949. Photograph by H. Rennison. Reproduced with acknowledgement to the Weekly Chronicle.

Newspaper cutting provided by Mrs Gladys Watson (née Cate) – daughter of Mrs Cate, manageress of the Rising Sun canteen in 40s and 50s.

Coal Fit For Kings
Written by Sid Chaplin, *Weekly News*, 28th June 1965

'The Romans in Wallsend had a name for coal, but probably never burned it. Their preference was for charcoal. One imagines that the smoke of charcoal burners' fires could be seen all around their fortress at the far end of the Wall. They could not know that 600 feet below their fortress was a seam of coal six feet six inches thick which was to provide the finest household coal In Britain. Wallsend miners call it the High Main. In a happy stroke of inspiration a mining engineer dubbed it 'Wallsend Best.' So high was its reputation that other collieries utilised the name, and soon there were coals selling as Blyth-Wallsend and Seaham-Wallsend. It was a coal fit for kings – and it went into kitchens and parlours all over the country. From 1778 to this day Wallsend coal has had an intimate relationship with the household trade.'

Acknowledgements to North Tyneside Local Studies, North Shields Central Library.

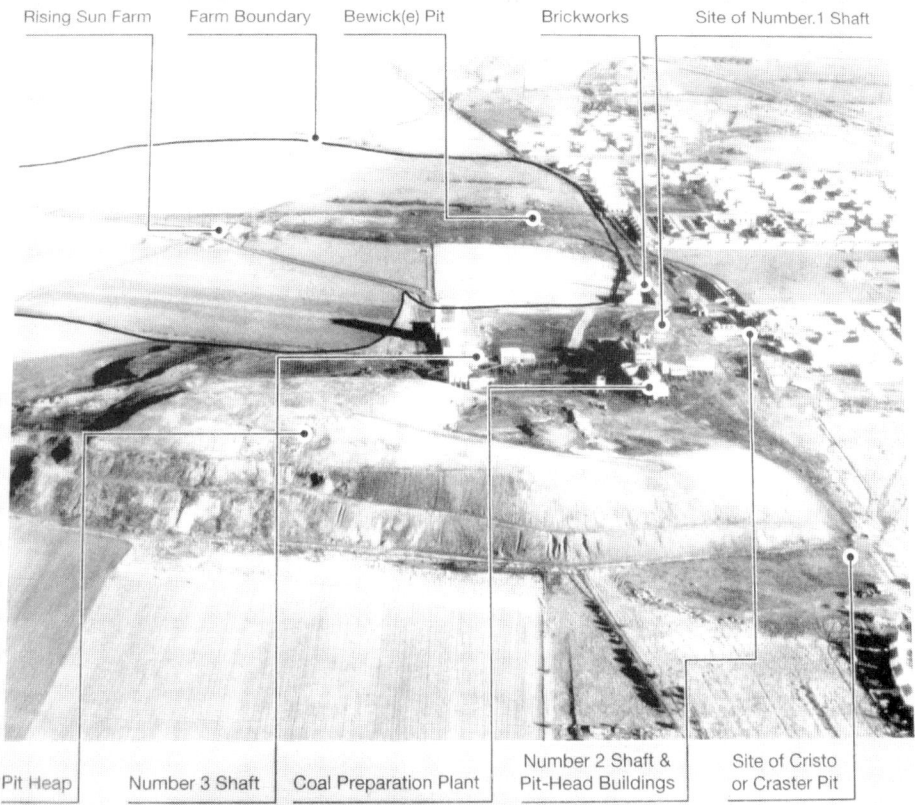

An aerial view of the Rising Sun Colliery.

As further proof of 'Wallsend Best' celebrity status I quote from *Views of the Collieries in Durham and Northumberland* by T.H. Hair first published in 1844 which states on page 10: 'Owing to the far famed prosperity of the colliery, the designation of 'Wallsend coal' has continued for many years a passport to the quickest sale at the highest prices ... Indeed, this favourite and important cognomen (Nick name) has been assumed with respect to the coals shipped from the Wear, the Tees and other districts of England and (even) Scotland'.

(We cannot get more famous than that, R.C.)

A very early view of coal mining in the area is shown in this sketch of Wallsend Colliery by the famous artist Thomas H. Hair. This image was first published in 1844.

The Early Years of the Rising Sun

This extract is from a brief history of the colliery in the Rising Sun Country Park brochure.

'The 1857 Ordnance Survey map shows nine pits in the area, but the Rising Sun which was opened later, was the largest and most modern pit. There was also a brickworks on the site (where my Uncle Harry Curran, an ex-miner worked) using the local clay. Work started at the colliery in 1906, and the first coal was produced in September 1908. It was a hot and deep pit and the smallest seam was the Victoria seam, only 0.45 metres (18 inches) high. The coal was gassy and sulphurous, so the danger of fire and explosion was always a risk. The pit was one of the largest in Europe, stretching under the River Tyne with 60 miles of underground tunnels. It was amongst the biggest in Britain. By 1931 the pit employed 2000 men. In 1947 (the year coal was nationalised) the pit produced 359,159 tons. In 1960 it produced 475,871 tons. Between 1953 and 1961 the National Coal Board spent over £2.9 million on modernising the pit to increase productivity. However, it closed within eight years when natural gas came into use, meaning gassy sulphurous coal was no longer needed. The closure put 1,180 men out of work and made 26 ponies redundant. Two hundred years of mining in the area finished with the closure of the Rising Sun pit in 1969. It is now a popular Country Park, the name of the Rising Sun lives on.'

The Price of Coal

There were around 30 major colliery disasters in Durham and Northumberland alone in the period 1800-1899 claiming the lives of more than 1,500 men and boys. Gas explosions were the major danger, although some incidents were caused by collapsing roofs and others by floods. The six worst disasters of the period in terms of numbers killed were: 204 killed at Hartley near Blyth in 1862, 164 at Seaham in 1880 (plus 181 pit ponies), 102 at Wallsend in 1833, 95 at Haswell in 1841, 92 at Felling in 1812, 76 at Burradon in 1860 and 74 at Trimdon in 1882. Colliery disasters highlighted the need for improvements in safety and as mines got deeper safety became more of an issue. The most serious of these was Hartley, which raised the issue of the dire need of a second shaft at all collieries as an escape route, but also to help ventilate the pit. Potential danger lurked every time anyone entered a mine, unless vigilance, care and physical measures such as dust suppression was installed. It is from this background that we arrive at nationalisation of the coal industry, not because of left wing ranters as some would have us believe, but because the coal industry was Mother Earth's own Dante's Inferno.

Right: *The Memorial to the 204 men and boys who last their lives in the Hartley Pit Disaster. The Memorial is the grounds of Earsdon Churchyard.*

Chapter 2
The Wallsend and Hebburn Coal Company

Before nationalisation and before helmets were worn and electric cap lamps. Underground workers pose at No. 1 shaft at the Rising Sun Colliery prior to going underground. Alfred Lee is the tall man second from the right whose brother John George Lee was killed underground in 1937. William Lee, his father, was employed as a filler at the Rising Sun. At the time they all lived at Hebburn. None of the names of the other miners are known. Photograph kindly supplied by Bill Lee.

An interview and first day at work

I clearly remember the morning that my father took me to the Rising Sun Colliery for an interview for a job with Mr. Whiting the Colliery Engineer. I was fifteen at the time. The Engineer was the top man responsible for all work, materials and men who worked in any capacity of trade, be it blacksmith, plumber, fitter, electrician, joiner or bricklayer, above and below ground, although each trade had its own line of foremen and charge men etc. Mr Whiting was very pleasant and asked me what I wanted to be. I had no idea. I had worked on the buildings for two years with bricklayers and had I known then that there were bricklayers at the pit (and down the pit) I think I would have opted for that. However, he looked me up and down and said that I had an ideal build for a blacksmith – and that was it. On the other hand had I known what was ahead of me I would have opted for the shipyards. In those days, thoughts of college or university was the equivalent of a journey to the moon. When I later asked my mother why dad had taken me to the pit, she said "It's a reserved occupation (no call-ups for the forces, she thought) and your father doesn't want you in the army. He's seen too much of it". It wasn't altogether correct. Many workers below ground were either called up or volunteered and quite a number returned to the pit after the war. That's actually what it meant. The job was reserved for those who returned. In any case, I still wasn't old enough for the forces.

The Blacksmiths' Shop

On my first day at work, which was a dark cold morning in winter (or late 1942) I slid open a door on rollers and behind that was a heavy canvas flap. When I pulled that aside voices shouted "Close that bloody door". I had forgotten about the blackout. When I as a chubby pale faced youth entered, it seemed to me like Dante's Inferno. From the darkness outside, to the blazing fires of the blacksmiths, the ringing of hammers on anvils and the shouts of the men joined in a clamour of noise the like that I had never heard before. There were nine large fires (not termed furnaces as in blacksmith legend) and numerous machines, and at the bottom of the shop was the burners and welders department, where the flashes of the electric welders hidden behind sheet metal shields, were as bright as anything seen during an air-raid. And it was the first time that I had seen an earthen floor, a deliberate policy I was told, to prevent hot iron lying on it bursting the concrete into little pieces. Almost all the machines were driven by belts that went around wheels attached to the wall on iron angle suspensions adding to the din. These wheels and belts drove the large drop hammer, the pick machine, the circular stone grinding (sharpening) machine and a drilling machine. There were also two large lathes where two fitters worked. Little did I know that I would work here (and a newer shop much later) for twenty five years.

   Eventually the foreman, Bill Purvis entered. By far the most colourful character at the pit was Bill. He was a man who used to fly into terrible rages when things went wrong. We always knew when the volcano was about to erupt when the peak of his cap was slewed around to the side of his head and he would literally charge into the shop like a pantomime figure onto the stage, bow legged and wearing blue overalls with a face as red as fire, spewing out foul language, stammering and hitting out with his verbals at all and sundry. Big strong men dived for cover, or picked up whatever tools were at hand, pinch-bars, hammers, or whatever was needed in an emergency, believing that this was such an occasion, and made a dash for the nearest door, not knowing what the emergency might be but prepared for anything. They were usually right. Telepathy should have been an essential part of their equipment, but failing that it was back to the Boy Scout motto, "Be Prepared".

The family of cats

We had quite a number of cats in the blacksmiths' shop over the years, but I don't think there can ever have been any other like Tom, a "mongrel" moggy if ever there was one. He was blue grey and long haired like a Persian cat but his coat was tatty and much longer. He appeared from nowhere one day and picked a favourite fireplace, only moving from there when the fire went out. He was quite bizarre. You have to understand that although the fireplaces themselves were very large, the fire was small and compact and very fierce. Sparks inevitably flew from the hot metal lying in the fire, sometimes white hot, and Tom never moved. He squeezed his eyes shut and turned away and you could smell singing cat's hair. If you pushed him out of the fireplace he jumped onto the anvil. And if you were working on the anvil and pushed him off, he jumped back onto the fireplace. So the men left him. One day he was on the anvil when one of the smiths brought a rod of hot iron out of the fire, placed it on the anvil and indicated with his hand-hammer where the striker had to hit, as was the practice. A sheet of sparks flew past the cat who just jumped from the anvil back to the fireplace. So the men hit on a device. If a small pool of water is laid on the anvil at the spot where the hot metal is laid, and immediately struck with a heavy blow, a crack like a gunshot sounded and a shower of white sparks cascaded outwards towards the cat sitting at the end of the anvil. It screeched and ran up the shop, only to jump up to another fire.

   Other smiths were kindlier and lifted him up and down as required. One day, another much cleaner black and white cat strolled in, as cats do, purred around men's ankles and was made a fuss of. We were plagued by rats and mice and cats were necessary and Tom was a great mouser. When he saw this rival he looked interested. The black and white cat, much more popular with the men, moved around without hindrance. Eventually it found a place near the drilling machine. Several months later, we arrived in the shop to be told by the nightshift that under no circumstances had the new kittens to be disturbed. These had established themselves between the coalcutting steel jibs stacked on the floor near the drilling machine, benignly watched over by their proud mother, the black and white, which was sitting on the drilling machine table. Ben, the driller, took over the role of protector. He was nearing retirement age and a very kindly 'grandfather' type person.

   I was told by the foreman to shift the jibs which required some riveting. Ben stopped me. "You cannot do that. There are kittens in there. They're only days old". I was in a quandary. If I took Ben's line I

Another sketch by Thomas H. Hair from the 1840s – this time showing the Air Shaft at Wallsend.

would end up with a confrontation. Suddenly I thought, surely if the manager was told about this natural phenomena, he would be humane enough to say "Leave them". But it didn't get that far.

A jib is a very heavy metal contraption which consists of two pieces of sheet steel half an inch thick, six foot long and about a foot wide and rounded at the top. Each sheet is riveted to bars of steel which acts as separators around which the coal cutting machine steel picks revolve. The inside is hollow and a four inch square hole cut in the top sheet to allow a tension bolt to be screwed. It took two men even to lift them onto the drilling machine. While we were considering the problem, a tiny black head appeared out of the square aperture. Then another until three black and white heads shoved their way through the hole to look at the great wide world outside. At that point I knew that there was no way that they could be shifted.

Geordie Hood Jnr, had been to the office for his pay, so it must have been a Friday and he must have been on night-shift. He was a welder who worked in the shop and came through the door with his bull mastiff, a young, eager looking, wet nosed innocent, sniffing the alien air of the blacksmiths' shop like a bloodhound. Geordie made for me (so he must have had a problem) and suddenly his dog stiffened. It had seen the heads of these little mites whose eyes were as yet scarcely open. There was a sudden hiss, and the mother of the kittens had arched her back like the Tyne Bridge with hairs. It was now standing bolt upright above the dog. Not only that, but mangy old Tom was also poised in the fireplace ready to leap at any time. We watched amazed, not knowing what would happen. Suddenly like lightning, the mother (who never seemed to have a name) leapt onto the dog's back, followed by mangy old Tom. The poor dog yelped with fear and flew out, his lead trailing behind him and with two cats clinging on his back for grim death. I never knew what Geordie's problem was because now he had another, finding his dog. As you can imagine, he never brought it to the shop again.

Foreman Tommy Hughes got to know about the incident and insisted that the kittens had not to be moved. I think that he had sensed that there was a general admiration towards the cats and that the act of pure animal protective instinct had appealed to all. I took one of these kittens home shortly after I got married. It was a beautiful black and white. There were no semi-Persians among them. We had a budgie at home and it was a great whistler but not a talker. We bought a toy budgie and tied it to the outside of the cage, hoping to get it to talk. But to no avail. After I brought the cat home I removed the toy budgie and tied it to a length of string to entertain the kitten. I was swinging it to and fro with the kitten leaping into the air. The room door was open and led onto the landing which was two floors up. The poor kitten leapt up, high in the air and missed and soared between the bannisters down to the bottom floor below. I was horrified! I ran down the stairs and the poor kitten was alive but shaking like a leaf. I brought it back upstairs and it hid away all day. It recovered and took its revenge. It used to leap up at the curtains and then slide down, its claws ripping into the material. Doreen was not pleased of course. Eventually the cat had to go and I very reluctantly took it back to its parents. But by that time I don't think they wanted to know. But I never forgot that incident or that family of cats.

Hair's sketch of the drops and spout at Wallsend.

A Strange Premonition of a death

One morning I was standing as usual waiting for the bus to take me from North Shields to Wallsend. Also as usual were a group of underground miners from our pit who always travelled at the same time. There would be about five or six in total. As I stood there I got a strong feeling that one of them, a small rather insignificant looking man, would be killed that day. It is the most unusual feeling that I have ever known, before or since. It was not a feeling of foreboding, nor was it a feeling of fear, but just a certainty that this would happen. When we alighted at Wallsend to begin our quarter-mile walk up King's Road North to the pit-head baths, I as a youngster, walked behind this group, and the feeling grew stronger as we neared the pit. I contemplated what I should do. I was not yet seventeen, and they were adults. Could I blurt out to one of them "Hi, mister your going to die today!" It would have sounded absurd. But if I had, what would have happened? I would possibly have frightened all the men and if nothing had occurred I would have been regarded as a stupid young kid. Even as we all entered the baths and having this absolute certainty in my own mind, I was tempted to go up to the man and tell him to go home. But I didn't. I clocked in and crossed the railway lines to the tub shop where I was at that time designated to work. We were all given the task to go outside (on a very cold morning) and unload tub sides from the twenty-one ton trucks.

 I spoke to Alex my young mate. "Alex, I think a man is going to be killed down the pit today". He stopped working and looked at me without saying anything. He was waiting for me to continue. When I didn't he said "What do you mean?" I told him what I had felt and without further debate he seemed to accept it just as a belief that could be either proved right or wrong. He was a philosophical individual. Nothing more was said about it until a couple of hours later when the hooter blew. This indicated one of two things. We could stop work as it was 'dinner time' or that the pit was being 'loused' (vacated) because of a fatal accident. It was only about eleven o'clock so Alex and I stared at each other. "Hey, yor right Ron, that's weird", said Alex. We climbed over the side of the trucks, the time now being our own, and I told him I was going to the baths to make enquiries. To put you in the picture, the body would be carried to the surface in the cage at No. 2 shaft and from there to the medical centre. A door in the medical centre led into the pit-head baths and it was my intention to sit near this door until someone came out. I would then ask who it was. I felt that to be my responsibility. Eventually the door opened and a man called Alfie Weddle who had once been a tub mender but was now a bath attendant came out. I asked him who had been killed and he said abruptly without pausing in his stride "It's a man from Shields". I raced to where Alex was showering, a tremendous hulk of a lad with shoulders like Garth of comic strip fame and as hairy as an ape. He was as hairy as I was hairless. He even had hair on the back of his hands. I told him what I had been told. He squinted through the soap suds and said again, "Hey Ron, that's weird" and left it at that. I made my way home in deep thought. Could I have saved that man's life. Why had I been chosen for that premonition, because that is what it was. When I reached home I told my parents, and they asked who it was, but of course I couldn't tell them. But the following night his name was in the local newspaper. The following morning the man I had suggested never appeared, then or ever again. And so my one and only premonition had been and gone without any apparent reason. But then, do they ever have one?

The Three Old Codgers

In the days before nationalisation, there was no defined age when a person retired. When I first started in 1942, I was amazed to see how many really old miners still wended their way from the lamp cabin to the pit-head with their oil lamp and descended into the depths in the pit cage. One man that I remember clearly must have been at least 75 years old. He had a crooked back and a pair of bow legs and his face had more creases than a road map. To be fair to management, they were given jobs such as driving an underground winding engine that pulled in the full coal tubs from the point where they were uncoupled from the pit ponies, whose job was to bring them from the coal face. Or clearing the main roadways of debris, such as bricks, stones and bits and pieces of engineering equipment. There would be about thirty really old men. When I asked about this sometime later, I was told that in 1939, hundreds of miners had received their conscription papers, and it was only later that they put a bar on miners being conscripted as there was now a shortage in the coalfields. The surface was no exception. In our blacksmiths shop alone there was at least three who appeared to be about seventy, and an old man working on the drilling

machine. We had what we termed as three old codgers, the oldest being over seventy. These three I will describe. They are in the photograph on the left and they are, left to right: Jimmy Finlay (the eldest), Bill Dishon and Harry Nathan. Let me start with Jimmy Finlay. One of the best of many stories about him was told to me by Tommy Guy, a welder on the cleaning plant. I went to sit next to Tommy in the pit canteen and apparently Jimmy had just left.

"Ronnie, you wouldn't believe it" he said. "Jimmy Finlay just asked me what the stones were on my plate. I told him they were stones from the prunes in my sweet of custard and prunes, and he said, "Christ, I didn't have any in my prunes". He had obviously swallowed them whole without knowing. Those who may doubt the truth of this story, please read on. While I worked with Old Fin, a new chapter opened in my education. He was essentially a farrier or horse shoer, rather than a blacksmith pure and simple, although the two trades tend to overlap. The steam would rise from his head in clouds when he was engaged in a heavy job. He shoed the pit farm horse (the colliery owned the farmhouse up the lane) regularly and to see him peeling the bottom of the horse's foot, and then burning in the hot shoe to make it fit, and to smell the pungent smell from the horses foot (the protective soft corn under each foot that has no feeling) was an experience. But as lunch time approached (pardon me? We didn't call it that in those

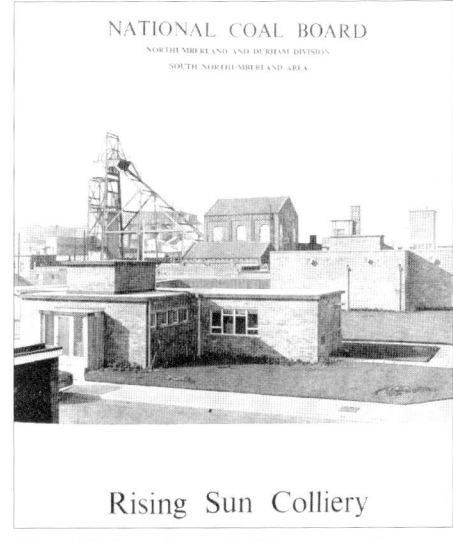

The Rising Sun Colliery on the front of this Coal Board brochure.

days) Jimmy would instruct me to cut a sheet of metal plate about eighteen inches square on the large steel cutting guillotine outside and fetch it back. He then placed this without washing it on the fire, emptied cabbage, rashers of bacon and two eggs on to it, and told me to watch that it didn't burn. He then picked up a very large bowl filled with a huge pie and carried it down the yard. I hurriedly asked Bob Kirtley the pick sharpener at the next machine, what I was supposed to do.

"Just turn them over regularly" he said. "He'll eat them, it doesn't matter what it looks like". Then he said "By the way Ron, do you know where he is away to". I didn't of course. "He's away down to the labourers' cabin because it has a big stove. He's putting his cow pie in there. He'll eat that after his snack on that plate". And Bob wasn't kidding. I saw it often. Old Fin's appetite was gluttonous. I had never before or since seen cabbage fried with bacon and eggs. I certainly had never seen a pie as big as these whole ones devoured by Old Fin. We called them cow pies, named after Desperate Dan of the comic *Dandy*. He was said to have another great appetite. And maybe that's why the ladies loved him. He was alleged to have a hut on his allotment within which was a couch where certain ladies of the town could visit at their leisure (and I was assured they often did) and some years later a replica of Old Fin might appear somewhere else in the town. One sixteen year old boy once walked into our shop. I was stunned at the likeness to Old Fin. With only a moustache and white hair (and a bit less of it) and there stood Jimmy of yesteryear. It was said, by those who knew, to be his grandson. This could well be true. Two of Old Fin's sons worked down the pit, one of them just like his dad but the other was much taller. Incidentally, it was well known at the pit that the underground miners all set their watches by the smell of Jimmy's fried cabbage circulating through the underground seams. At one time he had a cabin of his own at the pit top, and the downcast shaft pulled his nauseating pong down the shaft, through the pit and up the upcast shaft. It was said he liked cabbage. It seemed to be true. I'm sure it would be the longest journey of any cabbage aroma in the world.

Another character among the blacksmith's was Bill Dishon said to be a Frenchman. He certainly had the dark sallow features and his name wasn't English. He was the most surly man I have ever known. The boys called him Owld Dasher, which was the opposite to his nature. He played a violin and sometimes brought it to work and played it during "bait-time" (our definition of mealtime). I heard him a couple of times. It really was strange in that coarse environment to hear a violin playing among the anvils and blacksmith's fires at mealtime. Unfortunately and sadly, he was said to be playing it one day when he slowly keeled over. He died shortly afterwards. I was not on the appropriate shift at the time to see it happen, if it did happen at the pit. I worked with him for a spell during my apprenticeship, and can only say that his grunts (i.e. instructions) led me to believe I was his pet dog. He would suddenly walk out the door without saying a word. I would follow, only to find him going to the outside toilet. He would turn to me (this occurred on a number of occasions) and ask in a surly manner "where the hell do you think your going?"

I decided that I would not follow him if I could not get a clear message. Not long afterwards he turned and walked out of the door. Several minutes later he returned bawling incoherently at me. He apparently had wanted me to follow him on that occasion to the iron rack. I saw my foreman Mr Purvis and asked for another mate. Although to be honest, trying to tell Mr Purvis about it and listening to his reply, where every word exploded from between his teeth in a stuttering torrent of foul-mouthed abuse. I should have stayed with Owld Dasher.

Lastly in my catalogue of "Oldie characters" was a stranger who suddenly presented himself to the foreman one day looking for a job as a blacksmith. As he stood in the shop, a rare silence descended over the men. He was about sixty and grey haired and only of moderate height but so thin as to be able to say quite truthfully that he looked like one of the survivors of Belsen, the Nazi war camp where thousands died during the war. His head was literally a skull. (See picture on page 22, extreme right.) We could not for all the world ever believe that he would be employed, but we were wrong. He was given a test, which was to make six drawing axes, large wicked looking axes which were used to cut down the pit props underground. None of the younger men had ever seen these made previously. Not only was it a test of your mettle as a blacksmith, but also a test of strength. He amazed us all, with his dexterity on the drop hammer, his finesse on the anvil, and his general command of the tools of the trade.

Sinking a new shaft at Wallsend, around 1907.

He was of course employed. How could he not be? I was given a spell (which meant that I was employed as his striker) with this amazing specimen of a man – Harry Nathan was his name. He was promptly nicknamed Owld Nat. He told me that his physical problem was bleeding piles. One of his more demeaning jobs was to work with the tubmen in the field, cutting down tub sides and bottoms for future use. The tubs were the small metal trucks that carried the coal from underground, and if one "got bashed" in the process, it was brought to the tubs' graveyard where the good parts were taken off and used again. Much like a car scrap-yard. It was a very hard job, especially for the young strikers who had to wield a quarter hammer to chisel off the rivets and bolts, in each case. One day I had been sent back to the shop for some errand or other and when I returned, I couldn't find Harry. Eventually, I saw his head peeping above the rim of the tub. When I got near, I saw that he was praying. I felt quite embarrassed. When I spoke he started, and knowing I had seen him, told me that he was praying to die. He was sick of life, he said, sick of his wife who nagged him and sick of those who taunted him about his thinness. And sick of his illness. He then wiped his watery blue eyes and said, "Come on Ronnie, we have to get cracking". I felt acutely embarrassed but a sadness that I have never felt before or since.

I told Alex Allerdyce, one of my young mates and he said "Yes, I have seen him praying too". There is no doubt whatsoever that we had witnessed a man who believed that his life was so miserable that he would prefer death. It is hard to comprehend. However, one of the funniest incidents that I have ever witnessed was seeing Owld Nat, skinny as he was, chasing Owld Fin with a hammer. Apparently he had found that Owld Fin had used his enamel tea can as a dowser, in other words, dipping it into the filthy water of the bosh (the large water trough that stood beside each fire, which was used to dip the hot iron into or alternatively to scoop out water to dampen parts of the fire). The uncouth old bounder knew that it was somebody else's tea can, and he probably knew who owned it, but didn't care. The argument raged for about half an hour until someone shouted that the foreman was coming. An animosity lasted between them until Owld Fin retired when he was well over seventy. He was by that time seriously ill, although I don't think he realised it. I am sure he didn't.

Another character on the surface was Joe Wharton a yard labourer who worked in the labourers' cabin mainly making tea for the labouring gangs on the railway lines within the pit yard. Joe could be seen from about 11 am preparing for noon tea breaks in his tattered cap and gabardine raincoat fastened by a belt tied around his waist with about a dozen industrial tea cans attached, clanking as he walked. Even when they were full he would perform a St Bernard's waltz in an effort to preventing them spilling. It was hilarious to us young lads and just asking for cruel jibes. Poor bloke. When not making tea he was a yard shunter, a rather risky job when we watched him stick his shunting pole over the top of the buffers and under the central hook on the truck and sit on it as the trucks moved. These were huge steel twenty one ton coal trucks and he blithely jumped off and ran ahead of the trucks ready to hook the chain link over the next row of trucks. A very risky business. He used to go into a rage when we poked fun at him. I confess I was as bad as the rest because it really was funny. I am ashamed when I think of it now.

The Tub Shop

An early part of my apprenticeship was in the tub shop where tubs that conveyed the coal from underground to surface were fitted. The tub men used to race each other to see who could build the most tubs in a week, not for a bonus or extra pay but possibly currying favour with the gaffer. Riveting consisted of the tub mender heating a rivet until it was white hot in his brazier fire, entering it into the rivet hole, while I held a heavy iron instrument called a hobby which was pressed hard against the head of the hot rivet. On one very memorable occasion, this man in his urgency only half entered it and immediately started to bash in the other end. As a result it leapt out into my hand and immediately the smell of burnt flesh arose. I howled and dropped the hobby, whereupon in an apparent fury he turned to the fire, heated the pointed end of the tongs red, and lunged for my face, his teeth bared. I still can't believe he would ever have gone the full distance but in my fright I reached for the hobby and knocked the tongs away and made a swing at him. Later, the man made it known that he was only kidding, and perhaps he was but it gave me a fright.

Only the fact that I retaliated seemed to gain any respect. They kept well away from me after that. I was off work three weeks with a badly burnt hand. No one said a word to the foreman, not even me. When I was seventeen I developed a beat hand. Anybody who has had housemaid's knee or tennis elbow, will know about a beat hand. It is a condition where constant jarring and friction causes severe swelling and pain (in my case, striking with the quarter hammer and the much heavier fore-hammer) and unfortunately it turned septic. My hand had swollen so much that the fingers knitted at all the joints and turned almost purple. Eventually I had to visit hospital and when I arrived there I was asked how old I was. "Seventeen" I replied. "Then you will have to get one of your parents to be present if you are under eighteen" said the nurse. "You will need an operation under anaesthetic". And so I had to get my mother to attend. As we entered the hospital on my return visit a nurse was singing in the corridor the then top of the hit parade "You are my sunshine, my only sunshine, you make me happy, when skies are grey". My mother turned to me "There you are" she said, "That song is to cheer you up". I was off work for six weeks, the longest I have ever been absent from work. Although I returned it was against the doctor's advice. A scar an inch long from between the two middle fingers to the centre of the hand showed where it had been lanced. Loose skin now hung from my hand in large patches, and underneath was a new shiny red raw skin appearing. As you can appreciate, I had to wear a bandage and decided to go to work much against my mother's advice. However, I was hoping I would get sent home, but at least I wanted people to see that I was not shirking.

The foreman Bill Purvis asked to see my hand and then grunted "G'go over to the blooddy f'f'field and work w'with t'the tttubmenders". I was stunned. He was sending me back striking again. To their everlasting credit, hard men though they were, when the tub menders saw my hand they sent me straight back to the blacksmiths' shop. Of

The Coal Preparation Plant.

course I had to once again report to the foreman, and he curtly told me to work on the pick machine, another hand-jarring job. Was he just a typical lout of a gaffer from the old school, I wondered. I could not think of any other reason why he was so rotten to a young kid. Although having said that, the same man sent his adult nephew home for being an hour late in a snow storm. It was the heaviest snowfall for several years. The poor lad had to bicycle all the way from Washington in County Durham where he lived. And he was then sent home. How's that for savagery? It was Bill Purvis's wife's sister's son? Can you credit it? But it is perfectly true.

Changing the ropes

The most responsible, important and potentially dangerous job on the surface was the changing of the ropes on the pulley wheels, those great wheels above the shaft that draw coal and man-riders up and down daily. As you can imagine, not only have these ropes to be installed safely, but also at the correct length, allowing for stretch of these steel lock-coil ropes which were about one and a half inches in diameter. The person in charge of this was the cage smith. He was responsible not only for its safe installation but also for the renewal of the chains holding the cages, huge links about an inch and a quarter thick; and also the socket and its metal holder, which held the chains in place, each of which had to be examined for cracks, and in the case of the socket, ensuring that it was well and truly inserted. However, the man in overall charge of the total manpower on that day would be the foreman blacksmith. This manpower included: those on the very top of the pulleys, which was the name given for the meccano like structure where the pulley wheels rested in their metal 'shoes'; the men at the shaft below who dealt with every aspect of the cage, chains and the rope; the burner who burnt the ropes to length; the labourers straddled around the pit yard waiting for instructions; and those back to the wooden drum in the pit yard from where the new rope had to be carefully unwound in unison with the instructions from the shaft.

And the most unlikely man to be in overall charge at that time was Bill Purvis, our excitable, stammering, spluttering and panicky foreman, who created panic when none existed, like a one eyed bull, (yes, he had only one eye). He had people running in all directions, and on one notable occasion received a complaint from some of the women in the gaffers row, because of his offensive language, when there were many children in the vicinity. Of course, you had to shout to be heard at a distance. The length of these ropes were considerable from one end to the other, but it wasn't the shouting, it was the manner of it. The air was blue and purple and as one woman was heard to say, was there any reason for it? It took a good man to comprehend what was going on if you were somewhere among the motley gang of blacksmiths, burners, welders, joiners (they were required in the winding house), tub menders and yard labourers. On a freezing cold day, this was one of the world's worst jobs, waiting in biting cold for instructions to pull the icy cold and oily steel rope, and then wait again for the next order. On this job there was no hiding place and on most occasions, the colliery engineer would make his presence felt.

This was after all one of the most responsible jobs going at the pit, both surface and underground. Imagine a huge wooden drum sitting on a large wooden cradle around which was a 1 inch steel cable, at one end of the yard being unwound and man-handled along the ground to the shaft on its way into the winding engine house and around that drum and over the pulleys, the huge wheels around which the steel rope is coiled, over and down the shaft onto the top of the cage for final adjustment. About thirty or more men are involved from beginning to end and a mistake can be dangerous and costly. Yes, the cage smith's job is important. Likewise, so is the job of the shaft men. Unfortunately in one respect, the importance of mechanics and electricians, and indeed all colliery tradesmen was not recognised, following hundreds of years of a labour intensive industry from the coal face to the surface when coal was dug by picks and shovels, brought to the shaft by pit ponies and sent to the screens to have the stones hand picked off the belts. And of course, in earliest times, brought to the surface in baskets by boys and girls.

The Cleaner, as this Washery and Preparation Plant was commonly called, when it was opened in 1936. This colour wouldn't last long.

The cleaning plant that was built some six or seven years before I started at the pit, was a huge conglomeration of concrete buildings housing masses of machinery including shakers, chutes, sieves, a washery, metal belts and chain buckets, you think of it and it was there. This all had to be maintained on a regular basis, also to be repaired. Mechanisation came early to the Rising Sun Colliery. Linked with this new innovation there had to be of necessity, a parallel development underground, which made the Rising Sun Colliery one of the foremost mechanised pits in the country.

Remember When!

Left: *Another old photograph retrieved from obscurity – two of my old blacksmith mates outside the bolt store. Vincent Redhead (left) was a very good footballer and Bruce Black (right) a good friend of ours, who my wife and I recently 'rediscovered' upon their unexpected visit to Belford. They did not know we lived here, it's a small world. Frankie Hood, welder, is to the background extreme left.*

I last saw Vin Redhead when I and a friend met him with his wife in a club in Cullercoates about nine years ago. Although I promised to keep in touch I am afraid that circumstances prevented me from doing so, which was very unfortunate. I will try and make another effort. Vincent was a very good footballer and I am sure could have gone far. How it didn't happen is beyond me, but of course, in Wallsend the competition was stiff, as everybody now knows. Perhaps I could be saying had he followed a professional course, "I knew and worked with Vincent Redhead of Newcastle United?" Bruce and I go back a long time. One day he and I and Alex Allerdyce went to the Chillingham Road Baths together – three brawny blacksmiths going for a swim. We sat on the edge of the baths and confessed to each other, that none of us could swim. As we sat there the doors opened and a swarm of little lasses poured in from some local school and shrieking went to get changed. Within minutes they were in the water as we sat as though we were waiting for somebody. Suddenly Alex got up and said, "To hell, I'm going on the diving board". We watched open mouthed as he climbed the HIGH diving board and after shouting to the kids below to keep clear, he dived shouting 'Geronimo' and landed with a huge splash, sending a wave down the bath and the kids mad with excitement. Alex was no lightweight and if he couldn't swim I don't know how he dived into the deep end and arrived at the side of the bath grinning like a Cheshire cat. "I'm going up again" he said and he did. Bruce then did the honest thing and tried to swim. He was very tall and well built, a handsome blond, and the young lasses thought he was terrific. Alex on the other hand looked like a Gorilla, with hair all over his chest and arms and legs. His last fling on the high diving board was to beat his chest and give a Tarzan yell and jumped in with an even bigger splash than before. And what about me are you asking? I was trying to creep away quietly to get changed before these little'uns pushed me in for being the coward I seemed to be.

Alex and I were as close as brothers. I think that everyone at the pit thought we were. From the age of sixteen to 40 when I left the pit we visited each other, shared our fears, talked politics and football and of course work. I used to love to hearing him during dinner time goad his mate, Joe Husband, about Sunderland football team which he supported. Alex, totally football illiterate, would just say "rubbish" about any footballer Joe mentioned and Joe would reach high doe in a second. He would quote statistics, refer to the player's history, how many goals he scored, and after about twenty minutes blathering on Alex would then pull a Newcastle name out of the air and say something like, "He's not a patch on Albert Stubbins" to start him ranting again. Of course he did the same with me about politics. When I became a councillor for Tynemouth County Borough, he used to say "Aye, your on the gravy train now" knowing full well that it was unpaid in those early days. Had I not been single I couldn't have done it. Nevertheless, he still goaded me and I fell for it. Alex was passionate about his job. He seemed to have a natural bent for anything mechanical.

    I remember when Harry Thompson came to the pit from Ashington as the first trainee engineer I had met. Believe it or not, I had not been told anything by head office about their introduction, which meant attendance at Ashington Mining College, and an introduction into both fitting and blacksmithing, welding and anything mechanical such as locomotives, plant machinery etc. The first inkling was when the fitters objected to his 'intrusion' and he was sent to the blacksmiths' shop. The traditional tradesmen had their strong and long held views about 'one man one trade' so there had to be a special meeting of the branch. They decided to invite him to hear his case. At a packed meeting, one man who had been vociferous about him at the previous meeting, suddenly took a u-turn and turned to others as though they were to blame, and moved that we accept him and allow him to move between workshops. This was agreed, but I had learned a lesson that people can be very fickle and also have short, if convenient memories. However, Alex took Harry on in the blacksmiths' shop. He asked Harry if he could help him to work out an equation as to how to measure a piece of 1 inch square mild steel bar in order to make a drawing axe for underground. Making these seemed to be the ultimate task for a young blacksmith. Harry was delighted to be asked and, reaching for a piece of white chalk, he started first on the large black metal hood of the fire, writing an equation about three foot long. A group gathered and Harry found he had to move to the wall to chalk out his equations. To cut a long story short, Harry could not do what Arthur Waterhouse (a very good blacksmith) could do in his head, and although not admitting defeat, Harry could not give an accurate figure and Alex had made his point in the nicest possible way. Alex was another Arthur Waterhouse.

Chapter 3
Pit Ponies

Horse shoeing below ground

I served part of my apprenticeship with the underground horse shoer Bill Stewart, for about two years. One day I went with him to the Brockwell Seam stables, and on the way he stopped to talk to one of the roadway workmen. He told me to go on. I entered the stables which were in complete darkness (I did have my cap lamp however) and switched on the lights. The stable cat was sitting serenely on the top of a post in a stall, looking towards the mangers where the ponies feed was lying. There was a rustling in each stall because the stable seethed with mice. As the ponies trotted in after their shift, one by one, they first had a drink at the drinking trough, then trotted into their respective stall and proceeded to pick up a mouse between their lips, and throw them with a deft twitch of their head. The cat, immediately alert and waiting for this big moment swung into action like a world class goalkeeper. Never in my life have I seen anything like it. It was as though the ponies were in harmony with the cat. It leapt, pounced, clawed, and raced about the stable as though it was demented. After it tired of that it settled down to play with one unfortunate mouse. I'll spare you the gory details.

At our pit there were sixty pit ponies at the time that I worked with the horse shoer. They worked mainly in three seams, the Brockwell, Beaumont and Main Coal. Also there were about three other ponies working on salvage work in the defunct Yard and Low Seams. The ponies all had a character of their own. They were short, sturdy and very powerful and were very well looked after by horse keepers who worked three shifts. The horse keepers cleaned out the stables regularly, doled out the "choppy" (as the corn feed was called) into each pony's manger, filled the water trough with clean water, brushed down the ponies as and when required and examined the ponies for any injuries, and if so, sought from the 'putter' (the miner responsible for that pony) to ask how the injury occurred. One incident in the Main Coal Seam occurred to Soldier, a very long and larger than average chestnut pony. He had a large lump on his rump. The putter concerned was questioned about this but denied any knowledge of the cause. The horse keeper was suspicious and passed the matter to the head horse keeper who had the incident raised at managerial level. After an enquiry, it was confirmed by witnesses that this man had struck his pony with a 'dreg', a quaint name for a foot long piece of hardwood, exactly one-and-a-half inches square. He must have thrashed it severely. I heard that he was sacked immediately afterwards.

Pit Ponies at the Rising Sun Colliery, Wallsend. Photographs of pit ponies underground at the Rising Sun provided by Bob White.

This incident probably arose out of a habit of most of the ponies underground. They usually pulled two full tubs of coal from near the face to a point where they were then uncoupled and the tubs fastened to an endless haulage rope, which carried on the journey to near the pit shaft. These coal tubs were coupled with short chains each with three very large links, one linking to another tub and the other to the ponies yoke halter. The pony would stand and hear the first link falling into place, then the second. However, if it heard a third "chink", it knew that another tub had been added and refused to move. This was the putter trying a fast one over his mates and also over the pony. Hence the lashing every one assumed that poor Soldier received.

Another incident, also in the Main Coal happened while I was sent to look at the feet of the ponies still within the stable which was during the ponies' working shifts. There was only about three ponies in the stable, one being Sailor. The stable consists of two stables divided by a roadway between which passed the full tubs coming out on steel tracks (mini railway lines) and on the other side of the roadway, empty tubs going in. These full tubs were pulled up a slight incline by a haulage rope and the empties lowered down the incline the same way. Sailor was in the stable over the 'main roadway'. I heard the trotting of a horse and thought it was a pony coming "outbye" from the face, earlier than it should have. However, in trotted Sailor from "over the road" and serenely walked into Pilot's stall and started eating its "choppy". I stood amazed. After it was satisfied, it turned to the trough, took a drink and walked out, weaving between any passing coal tubs. Some time later the other working ponies started to finish their shift, and trotted into the stables, (followed by their putters whose job was to dismantle their harness and chains and the head helmet worn by every pony). Their harness chains rattling, they all stopped first at the water trough, then trotted to their own stall. Pilot turned up, took a drink, turned into its stall, and after a pause began to whinney. He then backed out and looking first to right and left, crossed the roadway and made for Sailor and commenced chewing at its mane savagely. How on earth did it know? I think it must have happened before. I learned later that Sailor could slip his neck halter with ease, having a slim neck. He must have also had a large stomach.

The most appalling accident to a pit pony that I know of (I didn't witness it) happened one day while I was still in the stable. Andy, a small, ageing grey pony was standing in its stall waiting for its 'mate' the putter. This man, called George Arnold, who lived close to me, was a very typical miner, rough mannered, using bad language like a guide to Saxon English, but with a heart of gold. He was one of the Jolly Boys, a group of miners who performed on the stage of the Miners' Welfare Club for the Old People's Treat each year. They used to dress up as fairies, and sing (but didn't swear) and the old miners and their wives had a great time. George Arnold came in with an apple and gave it to Andy. They had a great rapport. He 'dressed' Andy, said a few words to my mate and the horse-keeper and left for his job, which because of the age of Andy, was to do some salvage work on the roadway.

About an hour-and-a-half later the putter came dashing into the stable his face sheet white. "Its Andy" he garbled almost incoherently to Bill Stewart the horse shoer, "He caught his foot in the return wheel and its been pulled clean off". I reeled. Poor Andy having its foot torn off. That meant he was doomed. By this time the horse keeper had left and Bill had to frantically telephone to the surface. It was the job of the head horse keeper to sanction the shooting of the pony, the only humane action left. Old Bill Pears the head horse-keeper lived in a miner's house about a mile and a half from the pit at Willington Square. We used to see him with his stick, wending his way ever so slowly over the fields along past the pit railway into the pit yard, an old man when I first saw him. It took him more than two hours before he arrived

A pit pony at work near the face – pulling tubs of coal 'outbye' towards the shaft and then to the surface screens.

underground to see to Andy, who was then shot humanely after suffering the sheer terror of the accident. Meanwhile the putter was sobbing at the bottom of the stable. Bill Stewart told me to wait behind. He was going to rescue the foot, he said. He wanted to make it into an inkwell.

I couldn't believe what I heard. He later told me that as an army farrier during the first world war, it was a practice of theirs – due to so many horses dying on the field of battle – to use their feet and turn them into inkwells and other kinds of souvenirs. He had to wait until the end, when Andy was roughly tumbled into an empty coal tub and sent to the surface. What an ignominious end for such noble animals. In my time at the pit I will have seen about twenty such sights, a large bundle of horseflesh trundling around the pit to the surface in a coal tub, to God knows where. Some weeks later Bill Stewart proudly produced the final result. A foot scooped of its "corn", then polished and varnished black, with an insert of Royal Blue velvet within which stood an inkwell. Underneath the foot was a highly polished horseshoe.

Bill would enter a stable and when he went to examine the pony's feet, would give them a hard rap on their foot with his hand hammer, as they were quietly standing. The pony's foot would twitch upwards and remain that way quivering with pain while he did his examination. All he had to do with most of them, and sometimes did, was to place his hand gently on its shoulder and slowly slide his hand down its leg towards the foot. The pony would almost always oblige by gently raising its foot. Likewise, at the pony's rear, patting the rump and gently move the hand down the hind leg. One pony however was a very flighty animal. Its nostrils were permanently flared, its eyes bulging and red, darting quickly around from left to right, and its legs prancing and drumming the stable floor. It had a swastika branded onto its hindquarters and its name was Elwell. So from the very beginning it got off to a bad start with Bill. His First World War memories must have been stirred and he was determined he would 'tame' this animal. I think I should say at this point that pit ponies are, in my experience well looked after and well cared for by horse keepers and miners alike. My next paragraph shows hopefully, one of the few exceptions to that. To be truthful, if I had been the shoer instead of an apprentice, I don't know what I would have done with this particularly vicious pony.

Pelt the pony on the surface on sports day at the Rising Sun sports ground. Bobby Sansom is the Putter. The photo had almost disintegrated with age – now restored suitably for viewing.

Using a 'twitch' for the first time

For the pony Elwell, Bill used the twitch for the very first time while I was with him. This was a nasty piece of feudal-like torture which consisted of a piece of inch thick round wood about a foot long with a hole drilled through one end. A short piece of leather cord (or leather shoelace) was threaded through the hole and was tied to the other end, until it formed a loop. The loop was then placed over the top lip of the pony and twisted until the pony's lip quivered in pain. Any too active pony would usually calm down, its attention drawn to the pain in its swollen lip rather than its feet. But not Elwell. He pranced and danced while Bill used the very choicest words of the English language which even Shakespeare would have had difficulty to translate. It was obviously a battle between man and beast. "Here, grab this" he said to me, shoving this twitch towards me.

Having played no part as yet in this extraordinary battle of wits, and feeling that perhaps I could help the pony by unwinding the twitch, I took it and suddenly there was a loud thrashing as the legs of the pony stuck out in every direction. "Twist the bloody thing man" shouted Bill to me. All ponies were of course fastened to the wall and there was little chance of them breaking loose, but in Elwell's case it was straining backwards and I was really frightened that he would get free. I tightened the twitch. "Harder, man, harder" bawled Bill. Finally he said, "Give it to me" and twisted and twisted until Elwell fell to the floor. "Here, I've prepared some loops, drop them over his feet when I tell you". Cutting a long story short, Elwell ended on his back, with four feet in the air, each one tied to a stall handrail. He was shoed in that very humbled position. "I'll show the bugger" snarled Bill. Then in a quieter voice as though by way of an apology he said, "You've got to show them who is boss Ronnie".

Tank – built like a battleship

Another pony called Tank, in the Beaumont seam I believe, was built as his named implied. In appearance he could have towed the *Mauretania* but in effort he was totally workshy. I believe he thought he deserved the easy life and if you think I am exaggerating let me tell you the following. We went into the stable one day and he was lying down, a situation unusual to say the least. Nor could we get him onto his feet. So my mate the horse shoer decided to try and entice him with some biscuits but to no avail. We waited until the horse keeper arrived who examined him and could find nothing wrong. He turned and said to us, "Go out of the stable and wait a few minutes and I'll go to the top of the stable". We did that and within a few minutes we heard the scraping of horses hooves and the pony was hauling itself erect. We went in at this point and he just stood there like a truant from school who has been found out. But the worst of Tank I had yet to see. Every time we went to the Beaumont seam he was still in the stable.

Apparently it had got to the point that none of the putters or timber leaders wanted him, he was far too lazy.

One day when we arrived we found a putter trying to put on his harness but Tank moved this way and that resisting every effort he made. "Right" said Bill Stewart "I'm going to shoe you now. I've left you alone for a week but you've asked for it" as though the animal could understand him. He thereupon found a harness and with the help of the horse keeper put it underneath its stomach and hooked it to a girder in the roof. I was asked to help and we found a ratchet and slowly ratcheted this lumbering lazy animal until its feet left the ground. Bill then tied its four feet to the lower railings on each side of its stall, and then began to fix a shoe onto its feet one by one. I believe it knew it was being prepared for work and didn't like it one bit.

About a week later I was sent to the stable in the Beaumont seam by Bill who did his usual bantering to one and all and listening to comments on anything from the latest cricket scores to pit gossip. I entered the stable and was amazed to find Tank missing. Shoeing him must have worked. Later I heard a clinking of harness and thought a putter must be coming in early with his pony. However, I was astonished to see Tank on his own with his full harness on thumping into the stable and turning into his stall. He totally ignored me. A short time later Bill arrived and his mouth dropped. "It's no bloody good this animal, no bloody good at all. It doesn't even earn its choppy". I don't know what eventually happened to Tank but he was the most unpopular pony at the pit.

Right: *Ponies from the now closed Rising Sun Colliery put out to grass, their working life underground now finished. They are now enjoying daylight hours in the Rising Sun Country Park. Long may they enjoy their retirement. They certainly deserve it.*

A near fatal accident

As part of our routine, about once a week, Bill and I had to visit the defunct Yard and Low Main seams stables which housed only one pony each for salvage work. We reached these seams via a staple, a shaft within the pit which had its own cages, but no onsetter. An onsetter is a person who "raps you to bank" or to the bottom of the shaft, which means that he signals on a rapper bell to the winding engineman above when it is clear and safe to move the cage. There being no onsetter, it was permissible to "rap" what was called a man riding signal of three raps, enter the cage, close the gate and the engineman gave ample time for this. When he moved the cage it was with extreme caution. We arrived on this occasion at the Yard seam, walked several hundred yards in this deserted mine, until we reached a steep drift going up to the stables. Usually, Bill who was in his late sixties, would stop at the beginning of the drift, panting, and sit on a "kist" (chest) within which were horseshoes and nails etc.

He would then ask me to go to the stable and examine the horses feet and if I thought that they required shoeing, come back and tell him. Strangely enough, he rarely asked me to do it myself. He, like many of the older men, jealously held his trade secrets to himself or alternatively didn't trust a young lad. On this particular occasion he decided to go and have a look for himself. Pride, the smallest pony in the pit was a beautiful tiny piebald, dainty and sharp as a needle. Bill shoed him and told me it was his favourite. I was to see this lovely pony called Pride riding the conveyor belt in the Brockwell seam sometime later. It was a habit of the smaller ponies (the bigger and heavier ponies couldn't manage it) who, when their shift finished inbye, would jump of their own volition onto the running conveyor rubber belts to save their legs. They knew when to jump off. When Bill had finished in the stable, we made our way back to the kist to find in its place a mound of earth about twelve feet high. We had to walk over it up into the roof from where it had fallen. Bill would have been under it without a hope in hell chance of being saved. He went very quiet, very unlike him.

My time with the horse shoer was one of the most interesting periods of my time at the pit. To start with, Bill Stewart knew everybody, and despite his cruel streak to the ponies, was well enough liked. His humour was banter, where he would say outrageous things and get away with it. He often got on about my father "The old sod" as he would say. But there was no rancour or malice. Once he said of my father "To hear the old bugger talk you'd think he'd won the bloody Boer War on his own".

One day his banter went too far. We almost always travelled down the pit between shifts and the winding engineman (to give him his title) would always know when we entered the cage on our own. The winding engineman was the man in the winding house on the surface who drove the huge drum around which the ropes holding the cage spun. Bill had previously been in the winding house talking boisterously to the winding engineman. We were descending and upon the signal from the onsetter, the winderman dropped the cage at full coaldriving speed, which was three time faster than man-riding speed. He then stopped it abruptly at the seam level, and all the "G" forces roared through us as we shot up and down with the springing of the steel lock-coil rope. It was a horrifying few minutes and surprisingly frightened Bill more than it did me. When we eventually stepped out of the cage he immediately phoned the winding house from the bottom of the shaft and spoke a few harsh words. And when he reached bank (the surface) at the end of the shift he said to me "I'm going to give that bugger a piece of my mind!" I had no doubt that he would. But not only was it frightening, it was extremely dangerous. If a link in a chain holding the cage had snapped the effect could have been disastrous.

Above and right: 'Who wants a pony-ride?' Pilot the pony on Sports Day in the sports field with No. 2 pit shaft and the winding house in the background, in the mid 1960s.

Chapter 4
Early Days and Early Times

I stand to be corrected, but my recollection of the first manager when I started at the Rising Sun in 1942 was Mr Jack Thompson, although having said that I remember Mr A. Lawson who I believed at this time was the Agent for the area based at the Rising Sun office. This of course was before Nationalisation in 1947. I also remember that Mr Jack Thompson became area manager based at Backworth but I am unsure of the year. I do know that he still had an over-seeing role at the Rising Sun when I was secretary of the Wallsend Mechanics Branch from 1948.

Mr Jack Thompson, Manager at the Rising Sun Colliery.

Left: *Myself, Ron Curran, and Harry Hayes my striker, a Welshman just demobbed from the army. It is he who told us the story about the Ausies cutting off the finger of a sixteen years old Italian boy soldier on the Western Desert to procure his gold ring. That is not to say that our own blokes were perfect of course. War definitely changes people, hopefully not for life.*

The Wallsend G Pit – A Satellite of the Rising Sun

Wallsend G Colliery in 1910.

Although the G Pit had now exhausted its working life in producing coal, it was nevertheless an extension of the Rising Sun Colliery and was kept open through continual maintenance of staff from the Rising Sun and a permanent winding engineman. It combined a pumping station with an emergency escape route in the event of an accident at the Rising Sun, there being an underground roadway kept open and maintained for that purpose. I have received from Alan Brooks what I believe to be the authentic account of all the requirements of the G Pit as a satellite of the Rising Sun Colliery:

"The Wallsend G Pit is situated about 200 yards south of the New Winning Tavern on the south side of the new Metro Railway Line. What is known now as the G Pit comprises the G Pit (downcast Shaft) and the H Pit (upcast shaft) which contained an emergency/standby fan. The shafts depth were approximately 1200 ft to the Brockwell Seam. The pumping machinery was not a small incidental installation but an absolute necessity for a pit as wet as the Rising Sun. Water seeped in from many levels, from old workings of earlier pits in earlier times. The pumping station consisted of three Matthew Platt head turbine pumps of which one pump was always running; one was always on standby; and one was always under repair on a cycle. The Brockwell Seam water contained barium salt and iron oxide which fouled up the pumps internally and was a very time consuming job cleaning out the impellers, diffusers and the suction pipe range. As one can perhaps imagine, it was an extremely dirty and messy job for the fitters.

"The G Pit was manned 24 hours per day 7 days a week by 1 pump man and 1 winding engineman on each shift. The fitting staff usually working 6 or 7 days a week on day shift. Pit water was pumped up the H Pit shaft to a brick lined tunnel about 60ft from the surface from where it drained into the Tyne. This tunnel was inspected every 4th Saturday morning, via an access chamber in the North Eastern Marine Shipyard, by a team of 4 men including a deputy. The team went down the access chamber and walked back along the tunnel to the H Pit Shaft, and climbed ladders up the side of the shaft to get to the surface, not a task for the timid I would imagine.

Left: Ken (second name unknown), miner; Surface worker, name unknown; John Knowles, deputy; Alan Brooks, apprentice engineer. Photograph provided by Alan Brooks.

"For this visit both pumps were used and the standby fan was operated to draw air into the tunnel from the shipyard access. Apart from the actual inspection of the tunnel lining, 4 people walking through in waders against twice the normal quantity of water, churned up the yellowy orange silt deposit lying on the bottom, and helped to keep it clean. The smell of rotten eggs (sulphur dioxide) was very noticeable. The bottom half of this tunnel, from the North Eastern Marine yard to the Tyne outlet, was inspected about 3 times per year by the deputy only, at periods of very low tides – a very dangerous job. The problems with the mine water which occurred at the G Pit also affected the Rising Sun in a similar manner.

The Brockwell Seam

"The water here contained barium salts and was pumped out in a separate pipe range to other mine water. On the surface it went into settling ponds at the west end of the pit site, from where it was pumped overland to the Backworth Barium Plant. Here it was processed with barium water from the Eccles Colliery. The end product was a white powder similar in appearance to flour, which was taken away in wooden barrels. It was used in X-Ray work, film processing and paint manufacture. Entry to the plant was restricted and maintenance was done by the Backworth loco fitters whose loco shed and workshop was close to the plant."

Above information kindly provided by Alan Brooks former engineer and trainee manager at the Rising Sun Colliery.

Right: Bill Campbell, banksman; Jimmy Craven, labourer; Roy Kirtley, foreman fitter; Alan Brooks, engineers apprentice. Photo taken October 1957 and provided by Alan Brooks.

There would be few mechanics and electricians and other tradesmen who did not visit the G Pit during their time at the Rising Sun. It was a pit that required a lot of attention especially its water pumps that continually drained water from the Rising Sun. I think the G Pit could be called the first cousin to the Rising Sun. Or was it an Uncle?

The Edward Pit only appeared in my time as a covered bricked up shaft, when on occasions I cycled to the pit from North Shields. Many of the pit overmen and retired overmen lived in Willington Square including the aged Mr Pears, the head horsekeeper.

This is the row of colliery houses that many bus loads of passengers and car drivers must have seen in passing Willington Square on the Coast Road over many years. The houses were renovated of course and the pithead demolished.

Underground – Working at the sharp end!

Without any shadow of doubt the underground face workers were the front line of all trades and shades of industrial workers, working near danger with every living minute of the day or night. Roof falls, explosions, gas or flood were always a possibility quite apart from nasty accidents arising from working with tools and machinery in extremely cramped conditions. I include below information passed on to me while compiling this book. Anyone who hasn't been down a pit can never comprehend (even if they think they can imagine it) the difficulties of working in darkness lit only with small pools of light from cap lamps (it used to be candles) among loose stones, pit props and girders, often in water, and sometimes within the proximity of gas. Not only is it extremely difficult, it is also very arduous, requiring the stamina of an ox, the instinct of a fox for sensing danger and the stubbornness of a mule to get the job done. Quite apart from the dangers, for even just working in these conditions the miners deserved top wages.

Also if anyone has never even been down a pit shaft let alone going deep underground, are in for the experience of their lives. Even when one enters the cage and the gates clash shut, there is a feeling of finality to it. As the cage drops and you look down at the floor, it is possible to see a tiny light at the shaft bottom because of the many two inch holes perforating the bottom of the cage. This is to lessen the wind pressure under the cage as it descends. If you dare to continue looking you will see the light growing large and begin to hear the noises of underground, clashing and banging from below. To any newcomer, it will be with relief and surprise when they step out into a well lit and high area around the shaft, especially No. 2 shaft (which is an upcast shaft) with its high brick arch walls and roof about fifteen feet from floor to ceiling. This stretches in one direction for about twenty yards until it reaches the air-lock doors which trap and diverts the air. Beyond these doors we reach the six foot steel arch girders of the main roadway and the complete and utter darkness of underground. Your cap lamp may gleam upon the metal railway upon which the coal tubs carry out the coal. It is hard to believe that perhaps a quarter of a mile inbye, men are working at the coalface in confined spaces so low as to wonder how they can move let alone work.

And you would perhaps be surprised to meet a man working on his own possibly clearing stones from the roadway or some other odd job often given to older men. And don't be too surprised to hear the clink of harness and see a gleam of light from a cap lamp as a pony clatters past along the roadway with a 'putter' sitting on the limbers of a tram carrying timber for inbye. And you may have to stoop lower if the roof is now held up by timbers and props as you approach the face. You may even pass a group of stonemen fitting up roof timbers. And if you are really lucky you could be warned of a pending shot from a stick of gelignite shoved and stemmed into a hole drilled by a shotfirer who would be a few hundred yards inbye. You would have to hide in a recess built into the wall at intervals, until your hear the crump as the gelignite explodes. Listen to what our contributors have to say!

Alan Brooks was told in August 1968 to go down to a scaffolder's yard in Wallsend to examine the old A Pit shaft, sunk in 1784 and close to the ancient Roman Segedunum site. There were reports of ground movement and rumbling noises. The shaft was about 10ft in diameter lined with sandstone blocks and was flooded to about 100ft from the surface. Arrangements were made to fill it in using waste material from the coal preparation plant. This took about two weeks and it was then capped. This was very much a 'one off' job to make the area safe and prevent the collapse and cratering affect that old pit shafts can cause.

Bob White is originally a Jarrow lad who worked at the Rising Sun from 1956 until its closure in 1969, and then did a week on salvage work. He started on the screens on the surface and later went down the pit. He began in the Main Coal and it was very wet. He said:

"My job was to make sure the tubs were coupled together for the set 'runner' (a set is a number of tubs coupled together) to be sent outbye. Then it was my turn for stone putting working with ponies for the first time. Then my turn came for coal cutting on piecework.

"I really enjoyed working with ponies. Most of them were good natured and hard working. We used to share our bait with them but they just loved sweets. To name just a few of them they were Kettle who was really lily white, Frisk, Wisp, Aunty, and Don. After their shift they were hosed down and they really loved it, they used to roll over all over the place. I believe the stable keeper was Norman Patterson from

Coal cutting at the sharp end in a North East colliery.

Wallsend. Then my turn came for face training.

"The training centre was in the Low Main seam and it was the first time I had seen a Long Wall face. Halfway into my training the Low Main closed. The next training face was in the North Brockwell seam down No. 2 shaft where a machine called the Gusto Plough was being tried out. It would not work very well as the bottom (floor) was too soft, as I was told. Later on when I had finished my training I worked on a number of conveyors on face caunch work, until mechanisation came to the Rising Sun. My first conveyor was the West Winning Shearer in the Mothergate which was in the Brockwell seam. When in full flow I've never seen anything like it. It was blooming marvellous. After the Brockwell seam closed all the coal was extracted from the Beaumont seam until it ceased production in 1969. Why the pit closed I do not know? The last face I worked on was 715 Tailgate with Bobby Sansom and two other lads, Michael Kuchaski and Miraslow Hess, both Polish lads. I had a lot of good times working at the Rising Sun and I made some very good mates and I still have.

I always remember when I was face training in the Low Main after firing the shot and dressing the stone, we all used to sing, and it was always the same song, "There goes my heart". I didn't know the words but by the end of my training I did. One of the main trainers was Billy Gasgoine and his brother Phil was the deputy. At the end of the shift Billy used to give me his left-over bait but the other lads used to complain but Billy used to say, 'Bobby has further to travel' (to Jarrow) plus the fact Billy was from Sacriston the same county as me, Durham, it does make a difference. I had a lot of good times working at the Rising Sun, I enjoyed working down the pit. I would rather it had stayed open. Quite a lot of my mates left Wallsend and went to Nottingham to work at Cotgrave Colliery".

Left: *Underground workers of the Rising Sun Colliery in 1930. Acknowledgements to the 'Folks along the Road' published in 1980 by A. Senior.*

Bob White recalls some of those killed at the Pit: "In my time working at the Rising Sun there were a number of men killed. Jack Purdy was killed in a rock fall in the East Brockwell in 1963. There was also George Fatkin, Bob Kelly (who had been transferred from Seghill), Gilly Gracie (a filler) and Jimmy Bamburgh. I remember when I was in a queue with my paynote, I gave the lad my paynote number 1313, a voice from behind said 'Don't worry about that number son, it did me no harm'. He was right, a few minor injuries that was all. The man was called Rae Twizell. I kept my identity tokens. In fact I still have them".

   George Dixon, a former work study officer at the Rising Sun from 1964 to 1967 remembers: "I was part of a team of Work Study engineers carrying out work measurement on a Longwall Shearer face in the Beaumont Seam. It was the hottest face I ever worked on. An official told me it was 80° to 85° Fahrenheit and the humidity was very high. He said that the strata on that face was very hot and he didn't know why. Men on the face were stripped to their 'hoggers' (shorts), stockings, boots and knee pads. The men were all sweating profusely." George describes a system of draining methane gas through pipes from the face to the shaft to the surface. The pipes used at the Rising Sun appeared to be a range of 4ins or 5ins metal water pipes. "I was told that it was a methane drainage system that carried the methane gas to the surface where it was burnt off although I never saw where it was burning". But although he never saw where it was burnt off, nevertheless he said that the Rising Sun pit was the only one in his experience that had a methane drainage system, necessary it would seem because the Rising Sun was a very gassy pit.

   When I mentioned this to my brother Ken he said that Charlie Lumsden one of the older fitters at the pit said that the methane used to be burnt off in the shaft of one of the disused collieries, now within the site of Wallsend Park. George Dixon recalls the Cumberland William Pit disaster at Whitehaven where a terrific explosion was caused by a huge amount of methane gas accumulating high up in a cavity above the goaf. He goes on to say "I worked in a lot of pits in South Northumberland but never heard of a methane drainage system except at the Rising Sun". George Dixon believes that this could have saved the Rising Sun from a terrible explosion.

   Peter Thrower informs me that in mid 1967 while in training underground on face 22 in the Brockwell seam a lad "went through the disc of a shearer". This of course means that somehow, this lad was at the wrong end of a coal cutting machine while it was either running or turned on. His name is not known. One can only assume that this appalling tragedy was an accident that should have been avoided. I do not have a name for this unfortunate young man but George Dixon told me about the same accident.

   Bill Lee did not work as a miner. His brother John George Lee was killed in a rock fall on the face in 1937. I visited Bill Lee in Gateshead when he told me that his father William worked at the Rising Sun Colliery along with two of his sons. One of them was John George Lee.

The cramped conditions of a Northumberland Colliery.

Although this is recorded in the Durham Mining Museum records no further information is given. William's other son Alfred is seen on the photograph on page 16. This was provided to me from his own family album. He also gave me an interesting hour on the Primitive Methodists and their influence upon the mining community. I knew about this from information I received from my mother whose mother was born in Allendale where many lead miners lived and worked. Methodism was strong in that area but my own mother said that her family were Quakers. Not much difference I don't think, but I am sure that Bill could tell me.

    Charles Edward Brown was killed in roof fall. His back was broken and he died in hospital, aged 49 years, on 3rd May 1952. Information from Mrs Irene Molloy (née Brown). When I asked her if she was in any way related to Frank Molloy, who was a blacksmith at the pit, she said yes, she is his sister-in-law. When I mentioned this to my wife Doreen she then reminded me that we went to a young blacksmith's wedding many years ago which she believes was held in the Roslyn Hall in Stephenson Street, North Shields. She also said she has a photo of this. My wife has an amazing memory. I am sure this is young Frankie's wedding reception. We are looking for that photo. Isn't it a small world.

Robert Reeves was killed in an explosion. I was informed of this by Jeff Higginbottom who said that there is a memorial stone erected in St Peter's Churchyard, St Peter's Road to these men and others killed at the Rising Sun. None of these particular names are recorded in the Durham Mining Museum.

Matthew Gracie said that his father Gillie Gracie (married to Ruth), was killed by a shot by the shotfirer. (Shotfirers are men who bring down stone with gelignite to get to the coal.) Gillie Gracie had two other brothers, who with the help of Bobby Sansom, carried Gillie from the face to the shaft and stayed with him until they reached the surface. He was taken to the Newcastle General Hospital. The Death Certificate states: 'Died 25th February 1964, cause of death fracture of skull with brain damage'. The shotfirer was exonerated of blame as the fatality was not due to negligence by an individual.

George Fatkin was unfortunate enough to be the very last man killed at the Rising Sun Colliery on 10th February 1969. His name is recorded at Durham. He was killed in East Brockwell.

Jack Bamburgh worked in the South Brockwell and 'went over' the picks on the shearer coal cutter and was killed about two years before the pit closed.

Pat Lavin started as a putter underground and Pelt was his pony. He told me that there was an explosion when he was underground when only 18 years old in 1956 and remembers a whole seam of men being evacuated through an underground roadway to the G Pit near the riverside. This must have been a near thing for him and others. Strangely enough he was a near neighbour of mine in Laurel Street Wallsend about that time.

Robert Ryecroft (known as little Rickie) remembers a near miss of a possible disaster when he was sixteen in 1935. There was an electrical fault that affected the water pumps and gas pumps and the working of any machinery. Even the cages in the shaft could not move. He remembers being lifted three (men and boys) at a time in a bucket up the shaft to the surface along with another boy and an adult. He believes that their photos were taken at the time by Bob Waugh, of the youngest and the oldest boys and men going up the shaft.

Brian Allan, underground electrician, began his apprenticeship in 1942 and left the pit after 10 years in 1952. He remembers Jack Thompson as manager and Tom Green as under manager and also overmen such as Bobby Coulson, Jack Turner and the Williamson brothers. He goes on to say: "During my time at the pit, many Bevin Boys arrived and it was the first time I had met foreigners of my own age. It was quite a shock to my system going down a mine for the first time and I realised I was entering a world I did not know existed. I met many fascinating characters and made many friends. It was a wonderful experience and when in later years things got me down, I just thought of my experiences underground and everything seemed fine.

Hard work for this miner underground. Note the long handled axe lying across the steel conveyor. These were made in the blacksmiths' shop and used to chop down props underground. They were called 'drawing axes'.

"The normal cutting machines were fifteen inches (had a 15 cut) but there was a face in the Beaumont Seam too thin so we had a 12 cutter and I will never forget the night I was called to a fault in it. Feeling the earth slightly rumbling and having to feel my way along (I realise the size I am now I could not even have crawled into that space), it was quite frightening. The other most frightening conditions were the long-wall faces that were tried in the Main Coal Seam and East Brockwell where there was very little room to get inbye due to the bottom heaving. During my time at the pit I made many good friends. One was a boy from Scotland, Marcus George who was training to be a manager. I know that many people were disappointed when the pits closed, especially the men who had no other experience (except coalmining) but I think time will tell that no one should have to work in the conditions that we did."

Trevor Brown, underground fitter recalls when while working in the Brockwell seam on the 45 face the floor started to heave up and the roof closed down. Everyone was cleared out of the seam and the Mining Rescue Team were called. All of the conveyor equipment including the Anderton Shearer (coal cutting machine) and pans all disappeared into a void of gas below the seam. They lost everything but their own lives. He also told me about an accident that occurred in the fitting shop where a number of men were hurt including the foreman fitter Herby Williamson who as a result was off work a number of weeks.

Rueben Mason started as a timber leader underground and went on to become the youngest filler on the coalface. He remembers: "I was nearly 'happed up' (killed) when a stone fell on my back. After being taken to hospital I ended up at Hartford Hall the miners' rehabilitation centre. I was there a total of nine months. My father Bill Mason was a well known onsetter at the pit." Rueben was good enough to send me a copy of his Training Certificate, the very first issued at the Rising Sun Colliery. He has the honour of being the very first coal face trainee to qualify.

A picturesque view of Hartford Hall near Bedlington. It was built in the early 19th century and later became the Northumberland miners' rehabilitation centre.

Peter Allerdyce, while a putter underground, recalls the time in 1952 when his pony galloped forward and Peter became trapped between timber and his tram (tub). He received a pelvis injury and was off work several weeks. He also remembers Jack Purdy only 23 years old being killed, again with a shearer.

Billy Donald tells me that in the early 1960s in the Beaumont seam he and a number of his mates who he named as Geordie Arnold, Peter Allerdyce, John Curry, Walter McConnel, George Cook, Cud White, and Arthur Todd were filling on the face when the roof suddenly collapsed. There was four of the group at one end of the face and four at the other, and in each case they thought that their mates at the other end had been buried, as between them was a sizable part of what had been the roof. However, luck had been on their side and every one of the eight had survived without harm.

Chapter 5
Nationalisation
They Are Our Pits Now!

That was the general summing up by the lads – we now owned the coal industry. However, no one knew what that meant and what we were supposed to do. Surprisingly, the first thing that happened in our area was that Mr Rushworth, a former coal owner was placed in charge of the northern area of the National Coal Board. It was suspected, not surprisingly that this was also happening in other areas. In 1947 I was exactly twenty years old and involved locally with the Tynemouth Labour Party League of Youth and had been a member for two years. There was some talk about workers control in political circles but of course the Labour Government had no intention of introducing workers control. Unfortunately, mainly because of this, as elsewhere in other areas, miners took the view that nothing changes.

However, one thing did change. The miners' union was at that time named the Miners' Federation of Great Britain and had been so since 1888. But it was now felt that with a national employer, it made sense to match size with size, the employer and the union. In any case it would be impossible to be otherwise now because national agreements could only be negotiated with a national owner i.e. the National Coal Board by a national union, not the local coal owners as in the past.

Vesting Day, 1st January 1947, saw the nationalisation of Britain's coal industry. Mining communities believed this marked the winning of an epic struggle for decent wages, family security and public ownership of a vital resource. On that day miners and their families marched in thousands behind banners and colliery bands to the pit heads.

Left: *Three colleagues from the blacksmiths' shop with No. 1 shaft in the background: Left to right, George Sansom, blacksmith, (his uncle, another George Sansom was also a blacksmith who left a few years earlier), Michael Cain, blacksmith, Bob Kirkley, pick sharpener. Taken about 1950. Sorry about the dark shadows. I wanted the No. 1 shaft and pithead in the picture, unfortunately against the sun.*

Right: *Some of the blacksmiths, strikers, and welders who worked in the blacksmiths' shop at the Rising sun Colliery, Wallsend and with whom I shared a large part of my life. They were from left to right, back row: Wally Steel, George Sansom Snr, Bob Kirkley, Walter Cain, Ned Forster, Bobby Norman, Frankie Hood, Les Francis, unknown, Ron Curran. Front row, seated: Billy Pears, Tommy Hughes (Cage Smith), Jimmy Finlay, Bill Dishon, Harry Nathan, Jack King. Those missing are either on back-shift or night-shift.*

The photo above was taken in 1947 immediately after the Flag of the National Coal Board had been unfurled on No. 2 pit pulleys by our foreman, Tommy Hughes. He was also our union branch secretary.

"They cheered and some openly wept, as the blue and white flag of the National Coal Board was unfurled above them. They crowded round the unveiled plaques which proclaimed: 'This colliery is now managed by the National Coal Board on behalf of the people.' The dawn of nationalisation brought hope to the miners who had lived with the evils of privately owned pits all their lives. One could almost hear the cheers of heroes and heroines from the past as well as the present, celebrating the reality of public ownership".

An extract from the 'History of the NUM' Official version.

Automated mechanisation was introduced such as metal snake conveyors, Dowty props, and coal cutting machines with a circular disk wheel fitted with steel picks called the Anderton Shearer which, when it was laid out on the surface near the colliery workshops and viewed by all who wished to see, was pronounced by some as "Too big for the seam where it is intended".

Right: *Geordie Sansom ready to go underground, centre in the flat peaked cap. Other miners unknown although I recognise the face on the right.*

Left: A photo of the snowfall in 1947 taken in the village of Belford where I now live. I was discussing this particular snow blizzard with a friend in the local pub when he suddenly said, "I have a photo I can show you of 1947". He brought three. This shows the height of the snow which we had to clear in order that the colliery could remain open during one of the worst blizzards of the century. Unfortunately I have no photos of these conditions at the pit at that time.

One day during the terrible winter of 1947, officially stated as the worst winter on record of the 20th century, we arrived in the workshop to find that snow had blown in under the louvers in the roof, and was covering the floor, anvils and tops of the fires with about three inches of snow. Outside, snow was at least a foot deep and, where it had drifted, three feet and more, and it was still snowing. It was a fine and freezing snow, driven by a biting wind. We had all struggled to get to work that morning, through drifts and the buses had great difficulty in driving in such conditions. We all confidently expected to be sent home in such impossible weather. But we had all reckoned without Bill Purvis. He was in his element in bawling to us to "get shovels and come outside". We were stunned to say the least. We were led outside to the engine shed, and found that one of the "tankies" as we termed the steam engines was standing outside waiting to have a snow plough fitted. Some fitters and joiners arrived and we were then divided into teams. A number of teams were sent up the line to clear the heavy snow off the track in order to make the snow clearing easier for the engine, and the other team to fit the snow plough. I was on that team. What I thought to be the easiest turned out to be (or so we though at the time) the hardest.

We had procured spanners from the engine shed and in pairs, we had to manually lift the heavy snow plough, two at either side and place chocks underneath. Two others waited until the plough was high enough to enter the bolts into the respective holes and then tighten them. There were about four bolts on either side and what was a simple job under normal conditions turned out to be a nightmare.

The snow raged horizontally in the freezing wind, the tiny particles biting into the eyes that almost made sight impossible. Spanners were dropped by freezing fingers, and even Bill Purvis went quiet. He then indicated after only a few minutes, to swap the pairs around, and to go back and hide behind the wall, provided by the colliery office. It was here that men huddled in the most appalling cold that we had ever known. We then heard a whistle blow and dashed towards it not knowing what calamity it heralded. It was Bill Purvis shouting that half of us had to go to the canteen for five minutes to get warmed up. He nodded at a number of us and we dashed off as fast as we could. We couldn't believe that Bill Purvis had a heart, even in such conditions. But the day wasn't finished by any means. When the snow plough was fitted we were told to go back to the blacksmiths' shop and equip ourselves with as many pinch bars as possible. We were to be accompanied by the burners (the burner and welder was a dual job) who would take with them propane burners which was to melt the ice on the underside of the huge steel (21 ton) trucks that stood under the screening plant which fed the coal into these wagons. These steel doors fitted to the underside of the wagons and were held by a metal pin which was withdrawn to let the coal fall into the staithes down by the waterside at the river.

Our task wasn't only a terrible job, where the burner had to lie on the freezing ground in the blasting snow accompanied by a labourer or blacksmith whose job was to chip away the ice around the door hinges, but also a dangerous one with a full truck of coal (albeit iced up) above their heads. Others had to go along the track, again with a burner and defrost the points, they are the moving parts of the track that divert an engine and its trucks from one siding to the next. When we had finished the day, blue with cold and absolutely worn out and frozen to the bone, we were informed that the underground miners had been sent home due to the downcast shaft being frozen with icicles two feet long, hanging down them. They could have helped us I thought, somewhat jealously. However, pity for ourselves completely evaporated when those who had been sent up the track to clear snow arrived back in the shop. They were simply covered in snow, from head to foot and frozen to the bone. How they ever recovered I do not know. I have heard of bad winters since and some people claim that one of the winters of the 1960s was the worst. Not if they had experienced this.

Right: *Probably the engine to which we fitted the snow plough. The twenty-one ton coal trucks can be seen that had to be de-iced underneath to allow the coal to fall. Behind and above the trucks to the right can be seen the pit heap or what is left of it. It used to be the shape of an Egyptian pyramid but I am sure it was taller. It was certainly the most prominent of all the pit heaps in the area and there were many.*

One accident came to my mind at this time, which occurred during the excessively cold winter of 1947. An onsetter is a person who is permanently at the shaft bottom or seam, much the same as a lift operator, who "raps to bank" signalling to the winding engineman when the cage is ready to move to the surface. One rap of the bell for coal riding and three for man-riding. This determines not only the speed of the cage in the shaft but also the length of 'pause' before the cage moves. On this occasion, water or wet snow had frozen to the side of the shaft. A large slice of ice had dislodged and rocketed down the shaft striking the onsetter standing at the side of the shaft, stone dead. It was a totally unexpected accident occurring in appalling conditions. The bottom of No. 1 shaft was like an ice box. This shaft also acted as a downcast shaft that drew the air down the shaft and with it the weather from "upstairs" and through the pit and up No. 2 shaft, acting as a ventilator for the entire pit.

Left: A photo taken in the pit yard about 1950. In the picture are, standing left to right: Brian Readhead, blacksmith; Ned Forster, welder; Harry Hayes, striker; Wally Steele, striker; Jack King, striker; Alex Allerdyce, blacksmith. Kneeling: Joe Hayes Jnr, striker; Vincent Redhead, blacksmith. In the background is a small single-decker cage used underground in small shafts between seams. Please note in the right background, the primitive brick outdoor toilet with no windows.

The Wallsend Colliery Mechanics' Sick Fund

Along the way I introduced an innovation for our members, an insurance scheme whereby a member would receive a payment for each day off work over and above his normal sick pay, bearing in mind that national insurance sick pay was much less than a mechanic's normal pay. This was highly successful. We began by starting a local lottery at the pit, which was also successful, the proceeds of course going to the sick fund. We then had underground workers asking to join, and we agreed. The winner of the lottery received five pounds, which in the sixties was not to be sniffed at in the days of old money. Each member would then be entitled to £1 per week for each certificated full week's sickness or 10/- (half) for three days or over. The draw pulled them in. There was some criticism from a number of underground foremen who (this came via the miners' union) had suggested that it encouraged absenteeism. Anyone who was prepared to lose a full week's pay for one pound would have to be balmy. I was then approached at work by a representative of the Blue Cross Insurance company who suggested an injury benefit scheme for members of two pounds per week for one shilling per week payment. This included injuries sustained while driving a car. I didn't let on that we already had our own sickness scheme and said that I would ask around to see if there was any interest.

All I then did was transfer the names I had to the Blue Cross, and Lo' and behold we had a sickness and injury scheme for the price of one shilling, including the raffle of course. Moreover, the two pounds per week for injury benefit was a real winner. After all, nobody is going to injure themselves deliberately for that, are they? But there was always injuries at the pit, serious and not so serious. The Blue Cross rep was so impressed with the swift response, that he suggested including motorcyclists in the scheme. It really was lifting off. However, the motorcycle experiment was short-lived. This was the period when motorcycles were at their most popular and there were also many accidents and that part of it was withdrawn. But this scheme lasted until I left the pit.

We had quite a number of disputes at the Rising Sun. These often arose out of discrepancies between payments made to miners such as 'water money' for working in seriously wet conditions but not to mechanics of the mine, who had to repair the face machinery in the same place and under the same conditions as the miners. Additional to that, the miners had payments for 'waiting time', to make up for lost time while unable to work as they were paid a bonus arrangement. Let me say immediately that the miners deserved everything they got, but, I argued, so did we! But we were not disputing the payment to miners, only that they had to wait while a mechanic, or more than one, often in water, would work in the same conditions as the face workers without their recompense.

Right: Social evening on behalf of the Union Sick Fund at the Rising Sun Hotel, Coast Road, Wallsend about 1954. Standing, Alderman A. Sutherland, Mayor of Wallsend; Ron Curran, Branch Secretary Wallsend Colliery Mechanics; Thomas Cowan, Chairman. Seated at Piano Thomas Rogan, Treasurer.

A Two Week Strike

One day a young underground fitter came into the blacksmiths' shop to see me. He was ringing wet almost from head to toe, with coal dust glued to his face and clothes, and wearing Wellington boots in which his feet were sloshing in water. He was in a temper because, he said, that while he had been working for hours mending a machine on the coal face, the miners who stood or sat and watched were being paid 'waiting time' on top of their wages and also were being paid 'water money' for working in water.

Jimmy Selkirk, however, the young fitter concerned received no water money, only his day's pay. I asked him to come with me to the manager's office. The manager was in and agreed to see us. He listened in silence but said nothing. I asked what he thought and he said, "What do you expect me to do?" I replied that the least that could be done was to pay him water money. "He has to take these filthy overalls off which are soaking wet. They cannot be put in the locker so he has to carry them home where his wife will be expected to wash them. Surely that merits water money the same as the miners' get?" But, said the manager, they (the miners) had an agreement and we did not. This was one of the nastier spinoffs of modernisation. The miners had had a water money agreement for several years.

We argued, and he said he could do nothing about it. I asked Jimmy to take his Wellington's off and show the manager the state of his feet. He was soaked up to the kneecaps. His socks were drenched in water and caked with coal dust. The manager raised himself above the desk to take a peek and just said "Hmm". I was irritated at the lack of sympathy. Had he shown any I would have been more tolerant. I wondered what he would have thought if it had been his son? Jimmy and I walked out. I told him I was calling a committee meeting to discuss the matter as soon as possible. I did this and there was consternation. They made a decision to take strike action forthwith, because, they said, if they did not make a stand on this they would be rode roughshod over in future.

The strike continued into a second week and I was contacted one night by an executive committee member Jack Hopkins of Blyth. He told me that he had been selected to act as a mediator between those in dispute and the union executive – was there any way he could help? We tossed it around for a while, and I suspected that he was under pressure to produce something. Then he came out with it – the Coal Board was now threatening to sack all those on strike, as being unconstitutional to the rules of their own union and the joint agreements with the Coal Board. I told him I didn't know we had any, just disagreements.

If the Coal Board went ahead and sacked all those on strike, virtually our total membership of over two hundred at the pit, and if the executive, as seemed likely, allowed it to happen, and if other pits were not giving their physical support, it appeared as though our strike had failed. But if I said this to our men, who even now had high hopes of overturning the Coal Board, I would be seen to be surrendering under the slightest pressure and before we had really taken off, although two weeks is quite a long time in terms of a strike. It was a dilemma that I hadn't expected. I had led my members into this and I had to lead them out, with something. Hopkins phoned the following day, and our conversation turned around, by my instigation, if our executive abandoned our members, and allowed them all to be sacked, where would the executive stand in the eyes of the rest of the membership? Not only that, but the colliery would be standing idle with no mechanics and electricians to cover the machinery. "That's the Coal Board's problem", said Jack. He then said that the executive would, as soon as the strike finished, meet the Coal Board to discuss a payment for underground mechanics and electricians working on wet faces. He couldn't promise anything of course (well, that was to be expected!) and so we thrashed out a "form of words" that would hopefully satisfy both parties and give the impression that each side had won.

What we did gain, however, was a respect throughout the coalfield for standing up for a demand for fair play and parity with miners at the coalface, and creating a situation where our executive committee would be forced to seek a deal that should have been thought out beforehand in the first place. If modern coalmining meant anything, it meant teamwork at the face, equal partners with different roles but all part of coal getting and coal transporting to the surface.

A typical underground scene in a Tyneside Colliery showing the wet conditions men had to work in.

Rising Sun Reconstruction Plans Going Ahead

The Weekly News of 16th May 1958 reported:

"WALLSEND'S oldest industry, which had its origins in Elizabethan times and which during the last century gained the town world-wide fame for the quality of its High Main coal, is to receive a new impetus from the reconstruction scheme now being implemented at the 50-year-old Rising Sun Colliery. Although this is a long-term plan which will take some years to complete, there is plenty of evidence of what is to be the shape of things to come, both above and below ground.

New Winding Tower

The new winding tower will rise to a height of 115 feet above the new 22 feet diameter 1,400 feet deep shaft, which will contain multi rope friction winding gear similar to that already installed at Westoe and Ryhope collieries by the Durham Division of the National Coal Board. Following a Swedish design it will be the first of its type to be built in the Northern Division. The tower is to be built by October and the machinery is to be installed by March this year (1958). This will comprise two winders and two cages with counter balances, an arrangement which will allow the cages to be wound independently from two levels. Each cage will have two decks and each deck will carry two two-ton mine cars giving a total payload of eight tons per cage."

The No. 3 shaft, sunk in 1957. The brickworks chimney can be seen in the centre of the photograph and the No. 1 shaft is in the top right hand corner.

These plans were massive and costing millions of pounds. Anyone who had thought that the Rising Sun was only the poor relation would be more than surprised at receiving this legacy. That included me. We saw the construction of the new shaft taking place week by week by the Cementation Company who were the contractors building the shaft. Also the installation of surface machinery such as the huge Bradford Breaker, and the flattening of the pit heap, reputed at its peak to be the highest in Northumberland. Dumper trucks were everywhere and the pit canteen never had better custom.

No. 3 shaft from the inside. An entirely enclosed shaft-head where all the workings were weather protected.

Acknowledgement to Bob Stonebank electrician (shown above) for kindly providing this 'inside' information. The winding-engine house above, is on the top floor of this totally enclosed building that stands above No. 3 shaft. There are therefore, no pulley wheels or the traditional girder-like structure called the headgears.

New machinery was arriving in the pit yard almost every week, steel dowty props, also new conveyors and new coal cutting machines as the underground faces geared up for full mechanisation. New tipplers were being installed on the surface and new mine cars sent down the pit. New roadways were being built underground and perhaps it could now be seen why the 'new' mechanics and electricians had been sent from other pits that had closed. It now seemed to make sense. We could see the beginning of the end for most of the pit ponies who were currently being used for bringing coal from the face to the shaft. Conveyors had already been installed and made quite a number of men redundant but with full mechanisation only a small number would now be required for hauling girders and for salvage. For whom the bells toll!

Wallsend Mineworkers' Federation

The Federation as it was popularly called was an organisation at each pit where the various unions came together on common causes regarding local internal problems such as miners' coal as a case in point. This organisation was established in Wallsend on 13th May 1936. Each of the unions were entitled to representation. On Sunday 24th May 1964, 28 year later almost to the day, the Secretary from its inception, Mr George Sharp Young, retired, having given continuous and loyal service throughout. To honour that service, a special presentation with representatives of all the unions present was made and tributes given.

I wish to pay tribute to George Young and all men and women such as him whose guidance in life is from the heart and conscience and who instructs their head to follow that road. A more ambitious man may have crossed many more boundaries but would have had fewer friends. He was a true champion of the underdog.

George Young.

Prejudice

Things were beginning to come to a head for me in my job as a blacksmith. I was being given menial tasks when it was "my turn" to go behind the anvil. Alex Allerdyce and I had been placed together as blacksmith and striker to alternate week and week about. This was a situation that applied to no other blacksmiths in the shop, which many were newcomers from other pits in the area. I would be given a pile of tub buffers to stamp at the hammer (drop hammer) which entailed cutting out from cold metal sheets, certain shapes which when heated and then stamped would become the metal buffer which was bolted to the chassis of the tub. This job was purely repetitive and uncreative, and if I complained I would be given something much beyond my ability and experience. As for experience I gained little. I was used as a substitute striker for longer than any other apprentice. I was put on the pick machine, I was sent to the tub shop, an essential part of the learning trade, but kept there until I complained. I was then sent down the pit with the horse shoer, again part of the trade but once again I had to protest before I was returned to the blacksmiths' shop.

Alex Allerdyce (left) and I – at the Iron Rack.

A Wind of Change!

Inevitably retirement comes to everyone and it was now the turn of our foreman Tommy Hughes. Our previous foreman, Bill Purvis, who had been promoted to engine wright had retired some years before and I was now about to witness hypocrisy such as I have never seen equalled. A presentation of a gold watch was made to Tommy Hughes in the blacksmiths' shop, which was boycotted by most of the blacksmiths, strikers and tub menders with only a smattering of his well-known cronies standing around. Unfortunately, as branch secretary, I felt that it was an obligation to be there and nothing more. I was sickened when, after his friend Charlie Urwin, an ardent churchman made a treacly speech, and Tommy made a reply, the tears streaming down his face. A more bigoted and self-pitying man I have never met. When, as I knew he would, he visited us after his retirement, he made for the same cronies and probably made the same snide remarks as he always did. Indeed, on one occasion I actually heard him say: "That wouldn't happen if I was still here" whatever 'that' referred to.

But, as I have found over the years, new regimes mean new attitudes and very quickly Tommy became as much a part of history as Julius Caesar, however powerful he might have been. Soon even his cronies spent less and less time chatting to him, until we saw much less of him and finally not at all. Our new foreman was Joe Ward, until recently the cagesmith following the retirement of George Paterson. Joe was an effervescent personality, totally unlike what one would imagine a blacksmith to be, with a tall lithe figure, gingery hair and moustache, lively and humorous eyes and a sharp mind. When he first arrived at the pit some years previously, he quickly became popular with all the men. One night on backshift, he brought some paper clippings to work which included photographs showing himself and his wife winning the "Ballroom, Dancers of Great Britain" award. These were either in the *Sunday People* or the now defunct Sunday newspaper *The Empire News*. He was quickly recognised as a talented blacksmith and even the prejudiced Tommy Hughes could find no fault, and Joe replaced George Patterson as soon as he retired. By the way, I am not ruling out an element of free masonry, which was rife, but nevertheless I would have heartily endorsed his appointment, if I was ever asked.

With Joe Ward as foreman and Alex, now the cage smith and chargeman, I believed now for the first time that the slings and arrows of prejudice and bias would end and a new era begin. I was right, but please don't misunderstand me. Alex was forthright in his views and no one's lackey. Nor was Joe Ward a pushover and he had to be seen to be in charge, but his whole attitude towards the men was different to his forerunners. Nevertheless he hated when men took advantage of his easy-going nature; and became somewhat quiet and morose, which I am sure wasn't his intention. I never hesitated to tell anyone who needed reminding, not to push us back the clock to the old days of favouritism and bigotry. They never argued. Their memories were still too clear. I felt that I could now start to breathe freely with my work, which I still didn't enjoy much but I would make the best of it. And I decided not to emigrate after all.

My mates: Top picture left: Jack King, striker (left) with Alex Allerdyce, blacksmith. Top picture right: Stan Cole, tubmender (sitting) and Charlie Urwin (right). Bottom picture left, Alex Allerdyce (front left), with Joe Hayes, striker; Joe Ward, foreman blacksmith (behind left), Charlie Urwin, blacksmith. Bottom picture right: Joe Ward, foreman blacksmith.

The Pithead Baths

I understood from my dad that the Rising Sun pit head baths were built in 1937 at a time when a major investment was made particularly of the installation of a huge cleaning plant that cost several million pounds. The pithead baths and the canteen were a major step forward in improving social conditions at the pit.

For the first time, miners were able to bathe and change and afterwards travel home in a condition equal to other manual workers. This was instead of walking home as they had done for generations in the same condition as when they stepped out of the pit, often wet, and always covered in coal dust, carrying it into the home.

Right: *The colliery pit head baths.*

Accidents at Work

Two serious accidents occurred to blacksmiths while I was at the pit. I remember one occasion when I watched in amazement as a blacksmith using the drop hammer manipulated by a handle at the side by his apprentice, took off his cap and swept the scale off the hammer anvil, and just at that moment the heavy mechanical drop hammer crashed down and he lost two fingers, flattened to the skin. His apprentice who worked the handle had mistakenly moved it at the precise time that the blacksmith swiped it clean. George Sansom the blacksmith concerned was a neighbour of mine. He immediately hid his hand in his cap and I led him to the medical centre. He said he felt nothing but the blow and two of his fingers were flattened. George said to me "Jocka, take me to the Ambulance room" (Jock or Jocka was my nickname because my father, a Scotsman who worked at the pit for 37 years was a Scotsman named John, otherwise Jock.) As we walked over the crossing to the ambulance room he was berating the young apprentice. He was of course in a state of shock, but he never fainted or said he was any other than annoyed. At the ambulance room the nurse told him to look away and looked at the wound. Believe it or not he tried to make a joke. The nurse then turned TO ME and said "Are you ok, you look very pale". I honestly felt terrible. When I walked to the canteen to steady my nerves, I thought that Geordie Sansom was about the bravest man I had ever met.

A more serious accident occurred on back-shift, a shift that works the hours between 2 pm until 10.30 pm. I was at home when the telephone went and I was told that Billy Hetherington had had a serious accident on the Coal Cleaning Plant on the surface. It was feared that his leg had been severed. As an Accident Observer, a position established by the Coal Board in conjunction with the trade unions, it was a right of the union observer to attend the site of the accident, apart from the official Coal Board Safety Officer. We were allowed to take measurements and make references as we thought fit. I arrived on the site to find several sombre and sad men and officials. I was given the following information: Billy and his mate were 'breaking' a chain of conveyor steel buckets on a steep steel plated chute, using what is called a metal sylvester. This is a contraption with a chain which holds one end of the conveyor of about eighty large buckets while the other end is loosened to allow repairs. The sylvester chain snapped and the buckets spilled down and Billy, who had one leg overhanging the chute, had it cut clean off. He is then said to have directed operations by first asking someone to pick up his leg and ensure that it followed him to hospital.

This must have taken immense courage and grit. I visited him in hospital and he looked fine. He had asked the doctors to sew the leg back on, which they did. It would take some time, they told him but they expected him to use it again. In the course of time, Billy visited the 'shop' using two crutches. Then it was two walking sticks. Finally we saw him with only one walking stick. I am sure that had I stayed at the pit he would have thrown away his last walking stick – he was a little hero. But its amazing how life gives you another glance into the past. About five years later I was in my NUPE office in Newcastle when a lady entered the foyer and asked for me. She wanted to join the

The railway lines passing through the Coal Preparation Plant. No. 2 shaft is on the right hand side.

union. Apparently she was either a school meals person or a cleaner. She then told me that she was Billy Hetherington's wife, who incidentally I had met previously but not recognised. I was delighted to hear that he was by now in as good a healthy condition that a gammy leg would allow. About two years later I had a telephone call. I recognised that nasal drawling voice immediately. "Diya naa who I aam" said the voice. It was an accent from up the Tyne where Billy came from, having been one of the imported redundant tradesmen from the Isabella Pit. Yes, I thought, it's Billy Hetherington. But surely not … he wouldn't know that I worked here. Then I remembered his wife having visited my office about two years before.

"Is it Billy Hetherington?" I asked. "Yes Ron, it is. And y'naa what; Yid nivor guess that aam speakin' from the police station in Morpeth. I've got a job on the telephone switch board and aam phonin' up aal me owld friends to see how they're gettin on". I hoped he wouldn't get caught. I made arrangement to visit him, and Doreen and I spent a very pleasant day at their home in Morpeth. He had bought it, he said, from the proceeds arising from his accident. It's a pity he had to get it that way. I still often think of 'little Billy' and his awesome courage on that occasion.

My own accident – a very near miss!

I used to attend Industrial Injury Tribunals on member's behalf, sometimes not even armed with supporting medical evidence, arguing against the tribunal's representatives who were inevitably lawyers. Only when I became a member of the union's executive committee did I become aware, although I had been a branch secretary for some time, of the comprehensive scale of support available for the members, with medical consultants to refer to and lawyers to argue their case. There were no day or weekend schools on the subject and although I could have referred every case to Head Office at Falconer Street at Newcastle, it wasn't in my nature to send absolutely everything 'upstairs'. But one day I learned a lesson. I was taking up a case regarding a badly gashed finger of one of our members. It was clearly a very bad gash that I thought would have a future detrimental affect on his employment. He was a fitter. The chairman intervened and kindly said to me, "Mr Curran, are you aware that there are laid down rules regarding damage to fingers, even amputations that take every finger separately into account on each hand (depending upon whether you are left or right handed)" and I said "No." He then suggested, that with my agreement he would adjourn the tribunal and allow me to come back another time. I thought that was very decent of him. Yes, you have guessed right. I passed it on to head office in Newcastle where it was pursued successfully. After that, every case of industrial injury was referred to them. It is one of the finest benefits that unions have to offer.

I must mention my own, potentially serious accident where Providence must have intervened. The week leading up to the Saturday when Doreen and I were to be married on 14th March 1953, I was working on a metal gantry that I was constructing outside the 'heapstead', which are the group of buildings that surround the pit shaft. I was not able to set up a ladder because the railway lines for the 21 ton steel coal wagons ran very close, so during the week I used the standing railway wagons as a 'ladder' to reach my place which was virtually underneath the building. The purpose of this gantry was to be able to make it easier to carry out repairs on the underside of the 'creeper' that carried the coal tubs from the shaft to the tumblers that tipped the tubs onto conveyors and carried the coal to the screens. Between the row of trucks were stacks of pit props and timber leaving little room for any movement.

   This particular day I looked down the row of huge steel wagons to see if a locomotive was near ready to shunt the wagons down the line. There was none so I climbed upwards. I had just started climbing up the side of a truck when I heard a clang, clang, clang, the sound of the wagon buffers striking each other. I stopped and looked and just at that moment the wagon behind hit my wagon with a loud clang and I fell to the ground with the now moving wagons grinding along so close that I was only inches away. I rose to get out of the way, but was immediately struck at the back of my head by an oil box, a metal box about the size of a large shoe box which is filled with oil and attached to each wagon wheel. I was then terrified that I would be hit again in succession by each of the trucks as they progressed down the line. I somehow pressed myself out of the way in the very confined space and looked up, and saw an arm reaching down from the timber stack. It was one of the men from the heapstead.

   I grabbed his hand, and with the huge steel trucks still grinding past, being pushed by a heavy steam locomotive, I was hauled out of that death trap by the skin of my teeth. Alex Allerdyce my pal rushed to the ambulance room to see if I was ok, but no foreman appeared. It's strange when I look back to consider that the foreman never appeared, following an accident to one of his men.

   I attended our wedding with a large scar on my left ear which is clearly seen in the wedding photo and a very sore back and head. I also had a bruised left wrist which, in retrospect I believe was because my left hand struck the railway line as I fell. It could have been far worse. Even the minister was moved to ask if I required a seat during the service. Not on your life! Later I went back to view the scene and noticed that the railway line ran towards the timber stack to a wedge shape where only a cement pillar prevented contact with the pit props. The pillar was scored by the trucks scraping past over years. I also noted that the locomotive had been "up to the buffers" behind the wagons which was the opposite direction from what I would have expected.

Chapter 6
Welfare

CISWO – The Coal Industry Social Welfare Organisation

This organisation deserves some recognition as an organisation set up by the Coal Board to look after the welfare interests of the miners and their families. They organised exchanges between mining communities in different countries, encouraged pursuits such as music, art and athletics and generally worked closely with the established local Miners' Welfare organisations through their committees. My own personal experience was the setting up of a Wallsend Miners' Art Club through the agreement and support of the local miners' lodge. We were able to receive through them, six wooden easels for which I was pleased and grateful.

Miners' Art Club Exhibition

Wallsend News – 23rd May 1958

"An exhibition of water-colour paintings by members of the Rising Sun Colliery Welfare Art Club was opened on Saturday by Councillor Joe Branch, chairman of the Miners' Welfare Committee. The exhibition, held in the Welfare Hall, Station Road, Wallsend, is open for three weeks and is being held to stimulate interest among the miners in an attempt to increase the Club's membership. There are 15 paintings on view. They have been done by the Club's five members, 30-year-old Mr Ronald Curran, of Laurel Street, the founder; Mr Harry Plater, and his wife; Mrs E. Ferguson, a miner's wife, and 12-year-old Maureen Hedley, a miner's daughter. "The Art Club was formed in January," said Mr Curran, "and our aim in holding the exhibition is to encourage more miners and their families to join …"

"Two of his paintings in this exhibition are good examples of the use of water paint, and depict galleons under full sail on the open sea. Another, by Mrs Plater, entitled Lake Como, Italy, is striking in its simplicity, while Bluebell Wood, by Mrs Ferguson, is an artistic work with good perspective and depth. All the entries are clean and colourful subjects and there has been no attempt at abstract work. The Art Club hopes to be able to enter some works at the Wallsend Corporation annual show in September. Mr Curran, a blacksmith at the colliery, who has been painting since the age of 16, is a former member of the North Shields Triangle Club and has had two paintings displayed in the Newcastle Laing Art Gallery."

— FOR HIRE —

GRAND SPACIOUS

DANCE HALL

Good Seating Accommodation for Concerts, Political Meetings, etc.

Moderate Charges.

WALLSEND "G" and RISING SUN WELFARE HALL

Station Road - Wallsend-on-Tyne

An advert for the Wallsend 'G' and Rising Sun Welfare Hall from 1950.

The Inauguration of the Banner of the Wallsend Miners' Lodge

Right: Mr Willie Allen, Treasurer of the Northumberland Miners' Association, speaking at the inauguration of Wallsend Rising Sun Colliery Miners' Lodge new banner. This banner had been designed and painted by a young man whose father was called Bob Airey, a fitter on the cleaning plant. The meeting was held on The Green, Wallsend as the old village green of bygone days was called. My mother who was born in Wallsend and spent her childhood there, remembers playing on The Green with hoops and guards when she was a child. The speech made on the back of a lorry was preceded by a march through the town of Wallsend-on-Tyne, famous for the building of the Cunard liner the RMS *Mauretania* in its equally famous Swan Hunter shipyard and at the other end of the economic pendulum, king coal who had reigned for hundreds of years on the Tyne and in particular at Wallsend, its domestic coal being dubbed, Wallsend Best. It warmed the backsides of many rich Londoners for many years. And made many coal owners very rich indeed.

Left: Patrick Curran my father's nephew is holding the banner on the left of this picture. He was a member of the local miners' committee and lived in Wallsend. We called him uncle Pat but he was actually our cousin.

Coal was also the prime mover of the Industrial Revolution, being at the heart of everywhere that heating, lighting and steam power was required. It drove the engine house of Britain for many years on the backs of the sacrifices of miners and their families, in wages, conditions and even lives. It is no exaggeration to say that the term 'Great Britain' was created at that time from sheer muscle power, sweat and blood, not only of miners but also the navvies who built the viaducts, laid the railways, and cut the canals (and fought the wars). And it is at such times as inaugurations of banners and Gala Days that they should be remembered, with pride and admiration. If you are a discerning sort of person and like myself a bit puzzled to see that the picture on page 77 is not the same as the inaugural banner, so am I. However, it had to be a new banner after the sinking of No. 3 shaft because it is displayed across the banner in picture and words. But then I suppose, it was the business of the Wallsend Miners' Lodge and not the mechanics to either question or bother about the miners' own banner, although of course, all sections of unions at the pit gave way to the miners, either on marches or on platforms. It does however, show better than any other picture in my possession, No. 3 shaft completed and operating.

72

Right: Ian my brother is to the extreme right of the photo – you can just see his arm. He was a lover of pageant relating to the miners and attended most of the Durham and Northumberland Miners' Galas. Below is what we termed 'the colliery band' but what was by then Swan Hunter's Silver Band.

To say that a banner is a symbol is to say the least of it. When one sees the masses of miners and their families marching behind their village or town colliery band and banner at the miners' galas throughout the land and especially at our own Northumberland miners' gala, and the more famous Durham miners' gala, it is a display of triumph over adversity. It is a show of defiance against all the forces of authority railed against them in their demands for improvements in wages, better housing, safer working conditions, banning woman and children from working underground, and social justice in education and health. It is for these very human basic demands that miners and their families were pilloried by their employers and supported by law for many years.

Football and the Little Green Hut

Right: The Rising Sun Football Team, about 1954. I can only name one of the men and he is Walter Dodds extreme right at the front. He was given a job in the tub shop upon transferring from Hexham Hearts to the Rising Sun. He then was sacked by the blacksmith's foreman upon leaving to join another team. Fact not fiction!

The Interdepartmental Football Competition at the pit had been organised by a number of football fanatics, and the teams consisted of workers in all departments, both surface and underground. It was amazing the football talent that abounded. The blacksmiths' department had quite a good team and I was their goalkeeper. One of our players had been watched by Newcastle United and he played regularly for the Rising Sun Colliery Welfare. He was our star player called Joe Hay. But there were others like Vincent Redhead who also played for the colliery team. I had one major deficiency. I was small for a goalkeeper and found that agility was not enough to reach the far corners of the goalposts. However, we reached the final and won by one goal and I still treasure the only football prize I have ever won, a silver medallion.

    The 'Sun' as the football team was popularly known was run by Ernie Gustard of the green hut fame. This hut stood virtually at the entrance to the pit yard, a great vantage point for viewing any potential customer from his doorway. They all had to pass his door. This hut was a part of the Rising Sun's folklore. It was I suppose, the corner shop of the Rising Sun Colliery, almost living on the premises and stocking most of the essentials (in small amounts) from aspirins and Rennies tablets to tobacco and pepsi cola. It drew in all the characters at the pit, who visited on a regular basis for their baccy to chew down the pit, and in the course of so doing, would discuss everything from the football team to the latest local pit politics.

    I even suspected that loans could be extracted from the proprietor but that is mere speculation. Certainly I am sure that bets were placed here. Tommy Cowan, colliery electrician, was a regular visitor, to pick up any information about the football team or the Miners' Welfare Club, and so was George Gilchrist the Rising Sun's equivalent of the *News of the World*. Nothing but nothing got past George, to be sieved and sorted by his agile brain and then distributed at large as 'confidential' material. I was never sure of his job or what side he was on or who he represented. But like Lawrence of Arabia he always arrived at a place and time of particular import, with a piece of information as though it was worth having. The trouble was that most times you didn't know what to do with it. George would always leave surreptitiously with the aside, "Don't tell anyone that I told you".

The hut was also the equivalent of the *Newcastle Journal* for local hot news on almost any subject from cricket scores, winners of the Northumberland Plate, the placing of the local football team in the league and its strength and weaknesses, were all discussed here, to be later carried down the pit for general digesting. And all the while, the radio crackled and talked above the voices in this small corner of civilisation where I am sure that secrets were swapped, messages delivered, criticisms offered and judgements made. It was if you like, the fulcrum of knowledge regarding the past, present and future history of the Rising Sun Colliery and its inhabitants.

I myself was lucky enough to be invited to play for The Sun as their goalkeeper, I suppose on the strength of playing for the team that won the departmental pit trophy, but also because the North Shields YMCA for whom I played were playing The Sun at Smith's Park in North Shields and I was told I had played a blinder. I thought they meant I closed my eyes tight when the ball came towards me.

However, I lasted only one game for The Sun. We were playing at home, and in the first half I let in a goal, which turned out to be the only goal of the match. At the interval, Ernie Gustard the coach went around the team in the pit head baths with a can of beer or mineral water for each player. He walked past me as if I was invisible and I knew that was an ill omen. It was unfortunately a cup final and I had lost them the cup. He never picked me again, and although he knew me well by sight he never spoke to me again either. I even had to call at his hut at the entrance to the pit yard to retrieve my football boots but I never got them back. They had disappeared just like me. Perhaps they had been sent to the Hancock's Museum in Newcastle with the caption, "He Lost Us The Cup!" Nor did I ever play football again. It was an ignominious end to an ignominious career.

Right: Rising Sun Football Team – another time, another team. Sorry I cannot name all of the team. Back row: unknown, unknown, Wilson Price, unknown, John Bambrough. Middle row: All unknown. Front row: Kit Gibson, Pedlar Palmer, George Routledge.
I believe this was an earlier team because the coal depot and coal trucks can be seen behind.

Chapter 7
Mining Memories

The No. 1 shaft of the New Colliery, Wallsend in 1910 – the year that it was in the process of being built as the Rising Sun Colliery. The low building to the right of the middle of the picture would be where the tub shop was later built with the bigger building of the blacksmiths' shop yet to added. The buildings around the shaft and the screens are in the process of being built.

Past and present – A clever superimposing of the heapstead and pulleys of No. 1 shaft of the Rising Sun Colliery in the place where it used to be. Now it is part of the Rising Sun Country Park.

Memorabilia and Artefacts of the Rising Sun Colliery

Above left: The membership card of Ron Curran of the Wallsend Colliery Welfare Club.

Above right: Standing Orders of the Wallsend Colliery Mechanics' Association, Rising Sun Colliery, containing local and area agreements.

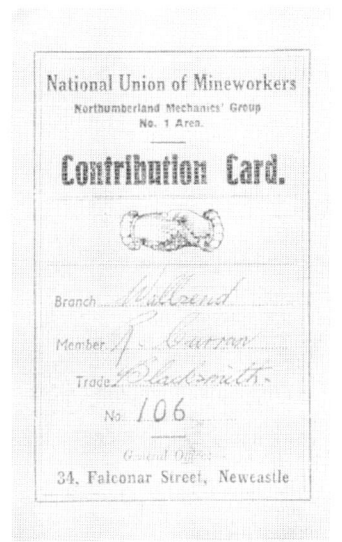

Above: The Membership card of Ron Curran of the National Union of Mineworkers, Northumberland Colliery Mechanics' Section, Wallsend Branch.

Left: Acknowledgements to Ken Curran for providing this photograph of the Wallsend Miners' Lodge Banner. You may have noticed that it is somewhat different to the banner that was earlier inaugurated on Wallsend Green. This must have been a new banner commissioned following Nationalisation in 1947 but after the sinking and opening of the No. 3 shaft.

Right: Two miners' lamps from the Rising Sun Colliery. To the right is the standard oil lamp which, if it went out could not be relit underground. To the left is a more modern lamp where a flash lighter could be inserted into the circular metal protrusion welded to the top of and to the right of the metal base. Contributed very kindly by Steven Allerdyce whose father was cage smith and charge man in the blacksmiths' shop.

Below: Pit Tokens necessary for going underground.

NCB Pit Token No 1517.

Cap lamp of Joe Ward, foreman blacksmith – for use in shaft examination.

Miner's underground token – NCB (National Coal Board) R.S. (Rising Sun.) No 1000. Thanks again to Steven Allerdyce.

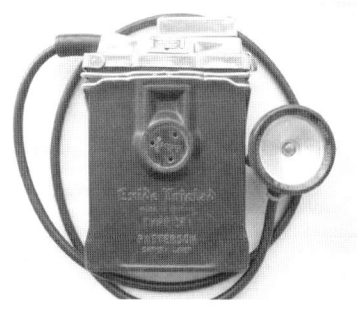

Miner's Cap Lamp R6551 – User unknown. Kindly contributed by Steven Allerdyce and family.

Tokens were issued at the Lamp Cabin to any person going underground, be it the manager, a miner or a visitor and the time of issue noted. This token is then gathered when they return to the surface by the Banksman then returned to the Lamp Cabin. Any token not returned by the end of shift, would require a search to be made.

Right: Reference from Joe Ward, foreman blacksmith on behalf of Alex Allerdyce, Cagesmith to "Whom it may concern". I am indebted to Steven Allerdyce, son of Alex Allerdyce (deceased), for this. Steven has provided me with most of the artefacts here, certainly enough to provide a chapter on the subject. He also has some amazing maps showing where coal has been hewed (with picks) or cut (with coal cutting machines) for over two hundred years. Hardly one acre of Wallsend Borough is immune from underground tunnels and the possibility of subsidence. Its heyday was the finding and mining of High Main Coal, the best and most productive of all the seams mined at Wallsend. This was the seam that made Wallsend famous. It's a pity that because of the size of these maps, they cannot be reproduced in this book. However, thank you again Steven for broadening my view of the volume of mining in Wallsend.

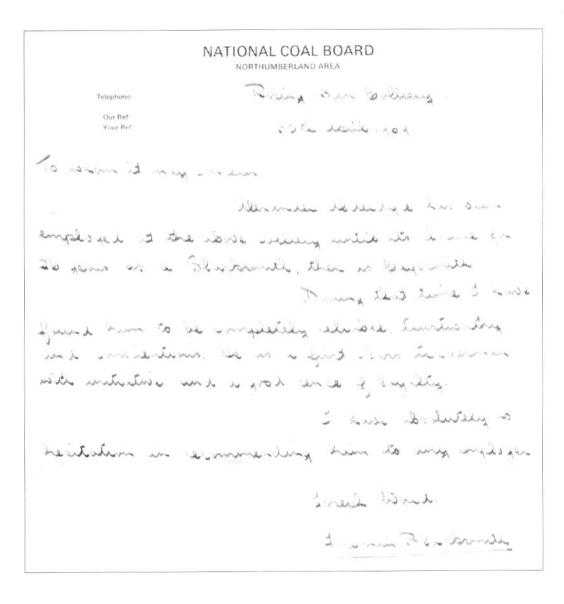

Right: This metal lighter was in the breast pocket of Trevor Brown's overalls when he was struck by a flying bolt in the 'new' workshop that housed all the tradesmen at the pit. The accident occurred in the new workshop in 1964 when Trevor was aged 18. They were slinging a machine in the workshop with a chain and the bolt snapped. The bolt struck his chest and knocked him to the floor. It could have killed him and he believes he was saved by his cigarette lighter (above with an indentation at the top). John Diamond was on the crane and Bob Brown on the pick grinding machine was knocked to the floor. Foreman fitter, Herby Williamson was slightly hurt requiring some time off work.

The pit lamp of Frank Hudspeth, deputy at the Rising Sun.

A Few Rising Sun Colliery Memories
by Bob Hamil

I lived in the Rising Sun Cottages from the age of 6 until the age of 23 and I must say on looking back I only have happy memories. Rising Sun Cottages was the row of pit houses which backed onto the pit yard. Below are a few memories of life back then.

Jack Hamil

My dad, Jack Hamil, started at the pit as a fitter, and ended up Unit Engineer. He stayed at the pit until it closed in the 1960s. As an engineer he had I believe to stay right until the actual closure, to make sure the site was safe. In my early years, I think in the 50s, the mines were becoming more 'mechanical' with the introduction of 'the Shearer'. I must say that the Shearer was not as popular, especially in our house, as the Shearer we know today.

With no phone in the house my dad had to rely on a pitman with a prop banging on our bedroom window in the middle of the night to let him know that there was a problem at work. More often than not, this was to tell him the Shearer had broken down. In the early days of mechanisation this was a regular occurrence and my dad would go days with very little sleep. As a family, we sometimes changed bedrooms around, so sometimes I had the experience of being 'knocked up' by the noise of the clothes prop rattling my window … that damn Shearer.

Jack Hamil.

Right: Unit Engineer, Jack Hamil's oil lamp inscribed with his name, with two models of coal miners. The left one is made of coal and the right made of metal. Jack's house, now the home of his son Robert (Bob) George and Sheila Hamil, is a marvel of memorabilia of the Rising Son Colliery. It is a mini-museum with models, certificates, photographs and maps, and of course Sheila's marvellous drawings of No. 2 pit headgears. Thanks for the memories.

Sunday Afternoon Visits

It was quite common for families to have a Sunday 'get together' after a hard week's work and we were no exception. Everyone would be in their Sunday best and my mam would have done the baking for the tea. The highlight of the afternoon, for male visitors to our house, was a visit to the pit. The visit would normally take in the time office, pit baths, blacksmiths' shop and the winder room. The real treat was the winder room … if you are into health and safety, don't read the next bit. The winder man would give us a demonstration of the workings of the cage (lift). This included the dead man's brake which was a means of stopping the cage if it should run out of control. He informed us that this was not a very popular way of stopping the cage when full of men. The men preferred their stomachs to stay just above their hips and not visit, be it only for a short while, their throats. The cage took the form of a yoyo in the shaft. The air would be blue when the men reached the safety of the top of the shaft.

Then there was the treat. As my cousins and I stood in our Sunday best we often were invited to take a trip down the shaft to see the ponies. The winder man always assured my dad it would be a slow run. The ponies had their stables at the base of the shaft and they were the cleanest stables I have ever seen. The ponies were well cared for having the best of food and they got first sniff of the fresh air the fan brought into the pit. The skill of the winder man meant we never had a mark on ourselves when we returned for tea.

The Lone Ranger

A friend of mine who lived in the 'cottages' was Michael Coulson. Michael was a little older than I was, and of the generation where sons followed dads down the pit. Michael had a job working with the pit ponies. The man and pony became great friends, after all they spent so much time together. One of the rules down the pit was 'You must not ride the ponies.' Lads of 16-17 years of age tended to feel this was a rule meant to be broken, and liked to get from the pit face to the stables at the end of a shift in as short a time as possible bare back riding.

According to Michael the manager took great pleasure in fining any lad caught riding the ponies. At the end of the shift the ponies sensed they were returning to the clean stables to be fed and washed down, and were as keen as the lads to get there, so they tended to trot. When they felt the fresh breeze on their faces, they needed little encouragement to gallop, and the lads needed even less encouragement to jump on their backs for the ride. A galloping pit pony took some stopping, so often the lads were caught by a gaffer and reported to the manager. Michael would have to report to the manager's office on pay day to pay his fine. The call was often heard, "Send the Lone Ranger in!" I'm sure the manager was hiding a smile and Michael didn't mind paying for his bit of fun.

The Rising Sun Colliery in the mid 1960s.

Bob The Copper

All the pits had their security man or 'pit copper'. Ours at the Rising Sun was 'Bob the Copper'. I must say us lads from the cottages made him earn his money. The pit yard was the best adventure play park any boy could dream of. We had trucks, coal tubs, massive piles of pit props, a pit heap, the pit yard baths, I could go on. We never did any damage, but boy did we have some fun!

We always imagined that Bob the Copper's job was to spoil that fun. He tended to wait until we were in full flow ... building a den in the props or racing in the tubs before he would appear. We would soon scatter and regroup for our next adventure after checking out who had got caught. On one occasion, I took a friend from school to play on the tubs. As was the norm Bob turned up. Unfortunately, my friend didn't have the experience of us lads from the cottages, and he got caught, whereas I took off, just like Jessie Owens. Bob the Copper, of course, handed my name in as the escapee. At tea that night there was a definite air of expectancy at our table. What would my dad say? He never had to say much, ever ... I always got the message. On this occasion it was quite brief, "You've been playing in the pit yard again ... (statement not a question). Bob the Copper says you're getting faster!"

I later went on to represent Northumberland at the All England Athletic Championships. So a big thank you, after all, to Bob the Copper for all that good training.

The Gold Mine (better known as Ernie's Hut)

The Rising Sun may have produced some coal over the years, but Ernie Gustard's Hut (shop) was a regular gold mine! Ernie had a little wooden hut positioned on the side of the road leading from the pit. From this hut Ernie would sell the men their cigarettes and tobacco. He had a book in which he recorded the tick the men had accrued ... no money passed hands until pay day. Then on Friday the men settled up immediately after getting paid ... so much for handling the pay packet over to the wife.

Ernie also found time to run the welfare football team. The lads from the cottages often helped him mark out the football pitch for the Saturday match. The pit sent over the sawdust and the lines were marked appropriately with a special mound for the penalty spots. Ernie had many more gifts than I, as a young lad, could realise. He did on many occasions oil and prepare my cricket bat, nail the studs in my football boots and lace up my size 5 'caser'.

The Local Chapel

I still remember my Sunday School Anniversary 'piece' from when I was four:

Down deep dark mines below the ground where fathers and brother toil
They dig for coal to warm our homes and make our kettles boil
God bless the men that dig the coal and work in cheerless gloom
And when the daily work is done, God bring them safely home

When my dad died in 2003, I had to inform the NCB. In my letter I finished off by saying that I was proud to be the son of a miner and that will never alter.

Right: This fine drawing of No. 2 shaft is courtesy of Sheila Hamil, the artist.

Sheila pays this tribute to her father-in-law, Jack Hamil:

"First he was married to Harriet, Bob's mam, at a time when their lives revolved around the Rising Sun and other pits in the area. He was a lover of his job. He was the gaffa, full stop ... apart from in the home, that was Harriet's job.

His second marriage was to Nancy who shared his retirement with him, and theirs was a different life altogether. They relaxed together and enjoyed the sunshine that had been denied him all those dark years in the pit. Jack Hamil was one of the most blessed men I know, because he had a special son. In his mind no other son could compare, especially in his sporting abilities as a lad. He was secretly proud of Bob when he outran Bob the pit copper in the pit yard, though he had to look displeased at the time."

It is People That Matter

Three mates – three coal miners. Norman Price, John Bambrough (killed underground in 1967), John (Pedlar) Palmer.

Pedlar Palmer and workmate Jozef Kozlowski (left) one of quite a number of Polish workers who came to the Rising Sun during the war.

Blacksmiths: Alex Allerdyce, Alfie Hagan and Harry Wilkinson at a union social.

Left: Three Rising Sun electricians enjoying a camping holiday in the sunshine. Left to right: Brian Allan, Kit Foster and Jack Leck. Kit Foster had two brothers who worked at the pit, one a deputy and the other a driller.

Brian Allan (left) and Dick Hargreaves underground foreman electrician in the old electrician shop on the surface.

Above: Alan Brooks as he is now. He is the young lad I recognise in the photograph of the G Pit wearing a helmet with a cap lamp on page 42.

Above: Three photos showing people enjoying themselves. Top picture shows Frank Hudspeth (right) with colleagues from the Coronation Club, Wallsend, believed to be on a trip to Seahouses. Bottom right shows young Neil Salkeld with grandma and granda at the seaside, believed to be Newbiggin-by-the-Sea. Below left is Frank again. Photos supplied by Neil Salkeld, grandson of Frank.

Right: Surface worker, Ian Curran, brother of Ron in 1949.

Bedlington – A Festival of Mining Families

Throughout the British coalfields a day was set aside in the miners' calendar in each area to celebrate their place in history as leaders of the British trade union movement. It is a day to remember the past but also to celebrate the future. There can be no doubt that the miners' struggle over several hundred years has passed down to later generations about the most ruthless of employers, and despite the law of the land supporting the coal owners, had thrown aside due to public outrage the employment of women and children underground. With the advent of nationalisation, born out of political alliance with the Labour Party, a new horizon appeared. The pits were now under public ownership, owned by the people, for the people.

The miners' galas held now in every coalfield once a year, epitomised the struggle of the miners for the last two hundred years for better and safer conditions underground, for decent wages that reflected the dangers of the job, the possibility of lung disease and therefore compensation as a result. And in the social welfare area of the miners, as many men became councillors to argue for better and adequate housing, better sewerage and drainage, lighting and clean water and all the facilities that would not only improve the lot of the mining families but also all people throughout the area. And no one can argue that their efforts were in vain!

The crowd listens to one of the speakers at the 1956 Miners' Picnic at Bedlington.

Marching through Bedlington on Miners' Picnic day in the 1950s.

The colliery beauty queens pass through Bedlington on the day of the Northumberland Miners' Picnic in the 1950s.

Frank Brennan

A famous footballer who was placed in a job at the pit was Frank Brennan, a Newcastle player who at the age of 22 years, was bought by Newcastle United from a Scottish team and also become centre half for Scotland.

Many of the miners employed at the Rising Sun were Newcastle United daft and when news got around that he was working at the colliery as a fitter, I am sure that more miners came to have their picks sharpened than hitherto. Just to have a close look of big Frank. Although he didn't work in our shop they might have been taking a long shot? I clearly remember when he arrived. I asked him to join the union, although it was only a ploy to speak to him as union fees were deducted automatically. He was 6ft 3ins tall and built like Gibraltar Rock. In fact that was the name given to him by the then Newcastle captain, Joe Harvey.

My younger brother Ken, a young fitter was paired with him for a while. Ken wore a smile whenever you saw him with Big Frankie. According to the Newcastle United records he arrived from Airdrie in 1946. He had been unknown south of the border until he starred in the Victory International against England. He marked Tommy Lawton (one of England's greatest centre forwards) out of the game and United had to move fast to get their man ahead of a number of suitors. With his size eleven boots he was a stopper in the true sense of the word. Indomitable of spirit, Frank's simple mantra was 'thou shalt not pass' and he either got the ball or the man. Keeper Fairbrother thought the world of him, claiming 75% of his success was down to the big man.

Ken was often seen with Frank, who towered over him. However there is one special occasion that Ken remembers well. Frank asked of him a favour. "Ken, I would like you to deliver a parcel for me and ask for a receipt. Come with me and I will show you. I have asked the foreman Tom McKend if it is ok." He thereupon took Ken into the pit-head baths and walked to his locker. He carefully took out a parcel and said, "I want you to deliver this to the Wallsend Town Hall. Do you know where it is?" Ken affirmed and asked "What is it?" Frank replied, "It's the FA

Frank Brennan in action against Arsenal.

Cup" and unravelled the parcel and Ken saw that it was still adorned with ribbon. Frank then wrapped it up and said, "Be careful and mind that you ask for a receipt." Ken thereupon strode out of the pit-head baths, with the future of the FA Cup in his hands. We can only imagine his thoughts as he arrived at the town hall and entered the reception. He asked to see the town clerk no less. "May I ask what you want him for?" asked the clerk with the wall of protection already being raised. "It's a parcel that I must pass personally to the town clerk from Mr Frank Brennan," Ken replied. Within a minute the town clerk appeared and invited Ken, with his blue overalls, into his hallowed office. He unwrapped the parcel with the cup and said to Ken, "Thank you very much and please thank Mr Brennan for his kindness. It is to go on display at our celebrations for the Festival Of Britain in Wallsend." It was as though he had been presented with the Crown Jewels. He clearly didn't care how Ken was dressed as long as he got his hands on the FA Cup. "May I have a receipt please?" asked Ken and upon receiving it returned to the more mundane stuff at the colliery. He had however, delivered a parcel that any thief on Tyneside would have given his right arm for, unless of course he was a Newcastle United supporter.

Ken went on: "A week or so later during Wallsend's Festival of Britain's celebrations on the Village Green I saw the cup on public display given pride of place in a big Marquee. The cup was guarded by a policeman as a huge queue passed by just to look at the cup."

Incidentally, the official report of Newcastle United states that Frank first went to Hartley Main Colliery, Northumberland as an electrician when he first arrived at Newcastle. Either they had it wrong or he worked at both pits but if he was an electrician he fooled everybody in the fitting shop at the Rising Sun. I should have asked to look at his union card.

Captain Joe Harvey lifts the FA Cup at Wembley after Newcastle's victory in 1951. Frank Brennan is on the right holding Harvey on his shoulders.

A Great Innovation! – Juvenile Jazz Bands

Above: The Rising Sun Colliery Legionnaires Juvenile Jazz Band in 1966. This photo is believed to be the original viewing of the new band and banner prior to the Wallsend Gala. This photo was taken by the *Wallsend News*.

The Rising Sun Legionnaires Juvenile Jazz Band was born during the awakening of youth within mining communities in the early 1960s. Jazz Bands were popping up all over Durham and Northumberland. It was great to see the children of miners all in colourful array, marching happily through their town or village with parents and sometimes grandparents proudly watching. Above is a photo which includes our own children, Susan aged 10, second from the left standing and Maureen aged 8, third from the left standing (smaller than Susan) ready to march into the town of Wallsend. We went to live in Dorset Avenue, Wallsend in that year and my wife Doreen joined the sewing meeting at the request of Mrs Bennet at the home of the band founders Harry Bennet and his wife. This was to make the band uniforms. My two children, Susan and Maureen were two founder members. This getting together involved the families in helping to make not only uniforms but also banners and much of the paraphernalia of jazz bands, also serving on committees and travelling and therefore mixing more often with neighbours. So the community spirit enveloped the northeast in a refreshing and important new avenue of its cultural heritage. This was the era of the children, sparkling and smart in their bright uniforms and showing the world at large their inborn pride in their mining background. Sadly the jazz band era suffered an almost fatal blow with the demise of the entire industry, closed down some would say by deliberate policy of attrition against the miners' union.

Right: The Rising Sun Legionnaires Juvenile Jazz Band, judged the best band on parade in the Wallsend Gala. Unfortunately I am unable to give a date – possibly 1966.

Left: This old photograph shows the Rising Sun band on parade in a local street. They trained on the sports field when the weather permitted and in the Wallsend Miners' Hall otherwise. They were trained by a military man as could be guessed by anyone who watched them on parade, from little tots to teenagers. I am sure that some will recognise a child or two among them, albeit 40 years ago. These are in the main, but not all, the children of mining families. I make no apologies for granting several pages for a review of the children of the past. These children are now in their fifties and perhaps older.

Right: On parade. The area has been suggested as near the Hadrian Hospital, Wallsend

"The best ten years of my life"
by Shirley Grice (formerly Shirley Sansom)

The Rising Sun Legionnaires Juvenile Jazz Band was formed in 1964. This was a really big event in Wallsend, particularly with the pitmen and their families. The recruitment took place at the old Miners' Club on Station Road (which is now Super Snooker). We trained on a Tuesday and Thursday night from 6 to 7.30. The venue was then changed to the old Drill Hall on Vine Street later to become the Community Centre. In the warmer weather and lighter nights we trained on the Rising Sun field which was brilliant, because nearly all of the competitions were out doors usually on fields. We loved it. These were probably the best 10 years of my life, as I retired at the ripe old age of 18. Some of my closest friends even to this day were involved in the band – it was our lives and nothing came between us and the band!

It taught us discipline and respect, and when John O'Shaunessy said 'Jump' we just asked "How High".

By the age of 14, I had moved through the ranks, from kazoo to being in the front row, and then my dream came true, I was made Band Major and Lynn O'Shaunessy was Drum Major. We felt so important, and everyone in the jazz band world knew us because we were the best! Happy Days!

Shirley Sansom.

Above: Shirley Sansom (centre) with Sandra and Rhoda Wilson.

Right: Shirley Sansom – Band Major.

Our Trip To Germany
by Shirley Grice

In 1971 we were invited to go and stay at the British Army Barracks in Dusseldorf, Germany. It was a twin town visit with the town of Rheydt. The road to the Wallsend Sports Centre is on Rheydt Avenue, hence the connection. The trip was to be for three weeks and the band was to be split into two groups – overlapping one week which was when the displays took place. We travelled from Hull to Rotterdam and took the ferry. I had never experienced sea sickness until then but I wasn't alone. Everyone was ill except one lad who was about 12 and he kept stuffing his face with chocolate – ugh! When we arrived at the barracks they seemed really vast and we had the run of the place, although only in certain quarters.

We did several displays for the soldiers, but on one very special occasion we were introduced to the Brigadier General. He came to me first and told me how smart I was and how impressed he was with the band having so much discipline. I was then invited to walk with him while he inspected the ranks. Nervous times! I felt a bit awkward because Lynn was Drum Major and she led the band but because I was the Band Major he thought it was my duty to accompany him. I was thrilled.

The Legionnaires on parade in Rheydt, Westphalia, West Germany, in style.

During our first week there, one of the older girls in the band spotted a soldier who she took a shine to. She really had it bad for him. They were introduced and she was in love. So much so that when we were due to go home after the first fortnight, she was given permission to stay for the third week. Love blossomed and within a couple of years they were married, and still are, so that the trip to Germany was meant to be.

We were all very upset to leave after our two weeks. It was a brilliant experience and wouldn't have missed it for the world. It was talked about for years.

Rising Sun Legionnaires proudly 'march past' in Rheydt.

Right: "Goodbye and thank you for your visit". It would appear that a presentation of goodies is being made.

Rheydt is an industrial centre; its manufactures include cotton, silk, and velvet textiles as well as machine tools, electrical equipment, and printing supplies. The city was heavily damaged in World War II. Nearby is the Renaissance-style Rheydt Palace (1567–81), now a museum.

On parade at the Rising Sun Sports Field with the pit heap in the distance.

Right: Receiving instructions. I am certain that the chap in the suit (above) is John O'Shaunessy. John was a fitter at the pit and a member of my union branch committee. And of course I did hear that he became very involved in the Jazz Band. In the front of the picture is Pauline Drew.

The Rising Sun Legionnaires in training, seen here at the Rising Sun sports field around 1963.

The Forest Hall Royals band appears to be marching in Wallsend.

The Rising Sun Colliery Whippet Club

This club was founded in 1963 and it is believed the idea of a club at the Rising Sun was conceived by a group of friends in the New York Working Men's Club who had among their members some miners employed at the colliery. Among those present were Jack (known as Pedlar) Palmer and Keith Swinney who in the course of time married Veronica Palmer, Pedlar Palmer's daughter. Keith and Veronica who I have mentioned elsewhere, have loaned me books and photographs for which I am very grateful.

Pedlar Palmer with his dog Pedlar at the Rising Sun Playing Field. Behind is a perfect view of No. 3 pit with what remains of the pit heap.

This photo is with kind acknowledgement to Veronica Swinney (née Palmer) and Keith Swinney, one of the founder members of the club.

The following information was given by Brian Renwick who, although himself not a miner, informs me that members of his family, who were miners, left this area to go to Whitehaven, Cumberland where they worked at Solway Colliery. He was also good enough to entrust me with a film of Wallsend Miners' Whippet club which was used by Tyne Tees Television for a children's program. Brian recalls: "Whippet racing started at the Rising Sun Welfare Centre around the early 1960s by a miner called Palmer, who had the nickname 'Peddlar', and a number of others. One old member rescued a whippet that used to hang around the welfare club house and aptly named it 'Club Member'. A committee was formed and the Rising Sun Whippet Club was underway. At that time there weren't many whippets around and the racing was a mixture of all kinds: Labradors, Collies and various others. The club met every Sunday morning at 10 am and as word of mouth got around it grew from strength to strength until there were twenty plus races every Sunday. The meetings soon became a family outing, especially in the summer when members would end up in the clubhouse for a drink and the handing out of the prize money.

"It wasn't long before the other collieries started their own race meetings and open meetings were arranged. Two or three busloads of dog owners would travel to Cumberland, Durham and Yorkshire to race against one another. It was not unusual for large sums of money to be laid between dogs of opposing sides. The outstanding dogs from the Rising Sun were Footprint owned by Brian Fenwick (so named because of a distinct footprint mark on its back), Gentleman Jim owned by Paddy Bowman, and Superdan, Iceberg and Iceblock. Around the mid 1970s a number of the miners decided to move down to Nottingham to secure their futures. This is when the meetings started to decline. Many of us still have fond memories which we still talk about to this day."

Jim Renwick with 'Footprint', a champion whippet.

Enjoying a day at the races are: Elsie Banbrough, Keith Swinney, with 'Pedlar' the dog, and Jack (Pedlar) Palmer.

Brian Renwick.

Two paintings by the author, Ron Curran. *Above left*: A whippet race. *Above right*: Following the 'hounds' at the Rising Sun playing field.

Chapter 8
Fighting to Save the Pit
Rocking The Union Boat?

I began my personal fight against pit closures in 1965 when I attended a conference of the Labour Party at Blackpool, as a delegate from the executive of the Northumberland Mechanics' Union. I was a little surprised that they sent me there but I suppose it must have been with the thought that I would be restrained 'from going out of line' within the ranks of the national body of the Miners' Union. However, whatever the executive thought, I was determined to carry the fight against pit closures onto the conference floor of the Labour Party to let THEM know that we were anything but happy. Within the industry we had been led to believe that if you could fight the good fight at local level. This meant increase production; to reduce ash content (being a pit that sent coal to power stations); to minimise absenteeism and industrial action; and work together to haul us up the league table as one of the most highly mechanised and productive pits in the area. Therefore it was a local battle in our own locality that counted, each pit having to fend for itself. In other words, profitable pits would be saved and highly mechanised high production pits would head the league table. However much one may despise this short term, law of the jungle policy, we were blaming the Coal Board for our current situation. I am afraid that as events proved, that was not the case.

As will be seen, I was very active within the union and was somewhat surprised at the rather luke warm attitude of the local miners' leaders to some of the proposals put forward by management. For example, when the manager said that it was now the policy of the Coal Board to change the economic evaluation of a pit's ability to survive, from being assessed on output, it was now to be measured in units. That is to say that the production per colliery per week was divided by the number of employees. In other words it was now productivity per head, whether a labourer on the surface, a colliery blacksmith such as myself or an office worker. What's wrong with that you might say? On a level playing field, perhaps ok but as a receiving pit from all 'airts and pairts' as the Scots would say, we were overburdened with miners and tradesmen from closed pits nearby. At one period we had over 20 blacksmiths at our colliery, along with more fitters, electricians and even bricklayers, way above what I would have believed a feasible and economic number. To give people a job who have been made redundant is ok in terms of social support, but only adds to the local problem and in the end solves nothing.

This belief was supported by Councillor George Eland (Secretary of the Miners' Lodge) unfortunately much too late, when he is reported in the *Evening Chronicle* of 30th January 1969, saying that "he personally believed that the greatest threat was the large manpower force involved. Men had been drawn from the Throckley Group, Mickley, West Wylam, and the North Tyne, Weetslade, Seghill and Backworth." Exactly three months later the pit closed. Nor was that the greatest threat. It just appeared to be another incomprehensible piece of administrative folly.

I think I was rocking the union boat at local level and I suspected that our union executive were trying to send me down the political route having nominated me as a parliamentary candidate rather than sending me to the Trade Union Congress or to the National Union of Mineworkers conference to which an executive committee member was sent each year. My reason for believing this was from what followed after being selected by them to attend a Labour Party Conference at Blackpool in October 1965, where I was part of a delegation of all the representatives of the National Union of Mineworkers.

I was not prepared to toe the national union line of playing cuddly with the Labour Government while thousands of miners jobs were lost. So I decided to try and catch the conference chairman's eye some time through the proceedings. The miners' delegates filled about seven rows of the seats in front of the camera. In the photo on the left I am seated at the front, third from the right. The union President Sid Ford, a bald chap is shown at the extreme right edge of the photo five rows up from my row at the front.

We sat right at the front of the conference hall as part of the large miners' delegation led at that time by the national president Sidney Ford. And I was determined to have some say about the closure of coal mines which by that time was a national issue. I was successful and called to the rostrum. I can remember the gist of my short speech because I had rehearsed it for several days. It went something like this: "Mr Chairman and fellow delegates (I didn't like the normal "comrade" form of address), almost every week we hear of another pit being closed, not because it has ran out of coal, but because it is deemed to be uneconomic. The benchmark for being uneconomic of course, is set down by the Coal Board in alliance with Government policy, which is set against the background of international competition.

"While we close pits in Britain we import cheaper coal from abroad, from places like Poland who subsidise their coal industry, and even from America who, it is said, can even sell it cheaper despite transportation costs. The American coal industry of course have seams of coal ten feet high as against our narrow and wet seams. But that has been the case for many years. Are we to allow this capitalist monster to kill off our only natural resource? (These were the days before North Sea Oil and Gas.) I do not accept that we are unable to protect this resource which is our only mineral wealth, and I will support this resolution which asks the government to review its fuel policies".

Our group chairman came to me as I sat down and said, "Mr Ford wants to see you. You have breached our rules by getting up to speak without asking permission". I ignored him. But I know that it was passed on to our executive committee. I had rocked the union boat. I did eventually go up the isle to see Sid Ford and he was rather puzzled. I wasn't apologising but said that I was unaware I was supposed to see him, but in any case I thought I had the right to speak on behalf of those I represented. He just moved his glasses and asked, "What is your name". I told him and then he said "Don't worry yourself" and that was it.

The Rising Sun - A Showcase Colliery

I remember when Patricia Medina visited the Rising Sun. To be honest, she was not a well known name but if she was deemed to be a film star, that was enough to grab the attention of the lads at the pit. On the day in question she actually did appear on the surface in the pit yard with a retinue of colliery officials so dense as to form an effective barrier against good viewing. In fact it was hard to make out a female when everyone wore helmets, a duffle coat and welly boots. She visited the stables. Pat Lavin and other lads were set on whitewashing the stable walls ready for the arrival of the actress; in the North East for the premier of one of her films in Newcastle. She arrived, according to Pat who witnessed her arrival to the stables, wearing the wellies of the manager's son, with of course, pit helmet, cap lamp and overalls. Upon seeing Pride, a tiny piebald pony, she bent and kissed its brow, whereupon the horsekeeper immediately chalked a ring on the pony's head around the lipstick mark stating, "That will never be washed as long as I am horsekeeper here".

Mrs Barbara Anne Allen sent two interesting photos of herself and colleagues visiting the colliery in January 1965. The visit was organised by the Coal Petrology Unit within the Geology Department of Newcastle University as part of a 'International conference on Coal Petrology' held at the University. She says that the visit to the coal face was an education in itself. (Never to be forgotten I'll bet R.C.)

Right: *Anne Dickens (now Mrs Barbara Anne Allen), centre, with colleagues from the Geology Department of Newcastle University pose in front of the pulley wheels and headgear of No.1 shaft*

Above: *Anne Dickens at the Rising Sun in 1965.*

The Day The Alarm Bell Rang!

Gloom started to replace cynicism as talk began about how long it would be before the pit closed? Then the gloom turned to pessimism, and the criticism for who or what was to blame became more open. Our's was a re-modernised colliery and its guarantee of a long future was underlined by the sinking of a new shaft and the pouring in of tons of new machinery and the opening of new roadways to service the newly mechanised faces. But, said the cynics, how does that square with all the re-dispersed miners and tradesmen pouring in from other pits that were being closed. We all knew that we were overmanned, a policy of the Coal Board to sweeten closures elsewhere, by offering jobs in a 'modern' colliery. There was also a growing pessimism throughout the industry at the new pressures being brought to bear about ash content in coal and cleaner coal being required to feed power stations. We were told that power stations were starting to call the tune, threatening to turn to oil. At the consultative meetings, we were shown graphs and tables and the future didn't look too rosy.

    I saw two main problems. One was the attitude of the National Coal Board to mechanisation. It seemed, and this appears to have been confirmed at other pits apart from ours, to have had a cavalier approach to mechanisation, by thrusting machinery at particular pits without consideration of local problems inherent in its geology – or if you like – horses for courses. The other was the lack of protection of a nationalised industry against other nationalised industries, who were making decisions damaging to each other, in other words there was no cohesive integrated strategy between them, although we had a Minister of Fuel and Power, an overall strategist – one would think.

I then conceived the somewhat desperate idea of putting myself forward as a candidate for Hull North as an Independent Miners' candidate on the ticket of Opposition to Pit Closures. With the death of the Hull North Member of Parliament, Henry Solomons, the two seat overall majority of the Government was cut to one. I know it sounds like political blackmail but an entire fuel industry was at stake, thousands of jobs at risk, and thousands of families would be affected. Moreover, the Government had reneged on its promises and I believed was conning the masses.

An unusual visit by Venezuelan airmen to the Rising Sun about 1964/5. This must have been organised by No. 1 Area rather than the pit. In the back row is Mr Potts, Area Manager, standing 5th from the left. The back row includes: Jimmy Green, Deputies and Shot Firers' Union, 6th from the right; Mickey Wafer, 4th from the right; George Sutherland, 3rd from the right; Mr Tait, Under Manager, extreme right. Front row seated: the Colliery Manager, Mr Haigh, is 6th from the left; Group manager, Mr Lewin is 3rd from the right; Ron Curran, Branch Mechanics' Secretary, seated extreme right; George Eland, Miners' Lodge Secretary, seated 5th from the right; George Jones, Secretary of Colliery Staff and Officials Union at the pit, seated second from the left.

I telephoned my Labour MP Ted Garret in Westminster and said I was coming down with two of my committee, chairman and treasurer, to see him at the House of Commons about an important matter. He asked "What is it about" and I replied, "Pit Closures". He then suggested that he could see me in Wallsend when he came up and he would listen to whatever I had to say. Ted was a very amiable man who I got on with very well. I had acted as his agent during the last General Election in 1964 so we understood each other, and of course I knew that he was in favour of the Government's fuel policy. There had been a recent Federation meeting at the Wallsend Miners' Welfare Hall which was packed with miners, mechanics and officials and where I had clashed with Ted on his analysis of the situation.

I am sorry to say the Miners' Lodge officials supported him, in affect saying that the Government were proposing a good deal in redundancy agreements. It was a meeting to hear the MP's report on the Government Paper on the matter. This was the day the alarm bell rang in my head. Bad enough fighting the Government without having to fight at home. Their 'head in the sand' attitude had worried me for some time, given that they were by far the most powerful union at the pit in terms of numbers at least. But their closeness in matters about fuel policy to Ted Garrett MP worried me even more. Ted, nice guy that he was, her was politically lightweight, not highly rated in Parliament, and certainly in agreement with Government policy on the coal industry.

To come to the point, I did not tell Ted Garrett of my intention to stand in Hull North, until I was promised to be given access to the Prime Minister. My two companions were Ken, my brother, who was now branch chairman and George Wharrior the branch treasurer, and of course myself as secretary. I had previously disclosed my idea to them at about 7 pm that evening and we caught a night train at about 11 pm at Newcastle Central Station. Looking back it sounds bizarre and cloak and dagger stuff, but I felt that the threat of a challenge to Labour's majority in the House of Commons might be enough to make them listen and think again about the colossal mistake they were about to make. We eventually arrived in London in the early hours and Ted then asked again about our business.

But I was having none of it until I could be told that Harold Wilson would meet us. But Ted was adamant. "Ronnie, you surely cannot expect me to demand that the Prime Minister meets you and I don't know other than it's about pit closures. What is it apart from that?" I then told him that if we could not get an assurance about Labour's intentions on the pit closures I would stand as an Independent Miners' candidate at Hull North in the coming by-election where, with the death of the member, had reduced Labour's majority in the House of Commons from two to one. I remember clearly his astonishment and gasping "Bloody Hell". Anyway he then asked us where we were stopping overnight and I said we had nowhere planned. He shook his head. "Tell you what, do you mind kipping on the Admiralty building floor. It's near the House. I'll tell the caretaker and cleaners and see you tomorrow". I'll bet he was wishing he wasn't. True to his word Ted turned up just before the rush of secretaries and researchers and whatever and took us for a wash and brush up. He then took us to a local café and paid for the breakfast. And do you know that he knew that I did not vote for him when he was selected at a selection meeting in Burt Hall a couple of years before to elect a parliamentary candidate for Wallsend. I voted instead for Jim Conway of Burradon the miners' nominee, but I hasten to add, not because he was a miner but I thought, the best man for the job.

However, Ted then took us to Downing Street and told us on the way that unfortunately Mr Wilson was so busy he has had to refer us to the Leader of the House, Mr Ted Short MP for Newcastle-upon-Tyne. I was gob smacked, but felt that I really could not expect anything else. There had been no appointment made, I wasn't a representative of the Miners' Union, only a branch secretary of a small union at one pit. (We had 206 members at that time.) I remember being shown into No. 12 Downing Street and meeting Ted Short who appeared very serious and sombre. He immediately got down to brass tacks. "I am told by the Prime Minister I can speak for him and wish to say that anything you say will be reported only back to him. I know that you are all Labour Party members (Ted must have told him) and I am sure you are as anxious as anybody that the Labour Party wins at the coming by-election. We only have a majority of one and if we lost we would be losing our majority. Let me hear what you have to say". We had previously agreed to have one spokesman and I told him we were concerned over matters that were occurring locally in our area and felt sure that it must be much the same elsewhere. There appeared to be expensive waste, over manning, lack of planning to match local strata underground and where as a consequence expensive machinery and seams were lost. And we wanted to know if there was an integrated fuel policy.

He asked us to put our concerns in writing and pledged that he would pass this immediately it was received to the Prime Minister. We felt we could do no more. On the way home

Former Prime Minister, Harold Wilson, on Horden Miners' Lodge Banner.

we assessed the situation. We all felt we could do no more and, in all conscience, we were lucky to have an interview. I then told them I had no mandate to stand for Hull North, no one behind me nor did the branch know anything about it. I said it was a bluff that might come off but if I had to go through with it on my own, I would, and I would ask anybody who felt the same as me to support me. I really don't remember whether our journey was over a weekend but I presume it must have been without missing a shift at work. We held a meeting at the Miners' Hall shortly afterwards and explained what we had done, and asked for their co-operation to write up a dossier to forward to the Prime Minister. Within a week we had compiled four pages and forwarded it to the Leader of the House, Ted Short MP.

Both Ken and Geordie asked if I still intended to stand as a parliamentary candidate and I said that it depended upon whether anything decisive happened. Besides, I wasn't at all sure that I would get any support from the National Union of Mineworkers. Probably I would not. When we returned to the pit, coloured helmets were everywhere. Red, white blue and yellow, rushing around looking important, some with clip-boards and others, possibly more senior, standing in groups. It was quite obvious that a red alert was out, someone had been very busy on the phone over the weekend. I sent the document and wrote about all of our concerns and a short time afterwards received a letter from Mr Harold Wilson, Prime Minister indicating that he was asking Mr Fred Lee, the current Minister of Fuel and Power, to have an immediate investigation. Meantime I called a meeting of the branch and told them what we had done, as an initiative on their behalf. I asked them to endorse this, and there was the usual "What are we endorsing?"

I explained that I was only seeking endorsement at this stage on travelling to London to try and meet the Prime Minister about the concerns within the industry. This was agreed unanimously. However, when we got to the "nitty gritty" as they say in the northeast, and heard that we had only met Mr Ted Short, there was a little cynicism, and someone quite rightly said "You could have met him in Newcastle". However, a committee member told him that if you don't try you don't get anywhere, and moved that we should be congratulated and that we could see from the activity – by all these bods in coloured hats – that we had stirred something up in the hierarchy. We then received their full endorsement, including the price of the train fare which we otherwise would have had to pay for ourselves.

I did not stand for Parliament and Kevin McNamara was elected to the House of Commons as MP for Hull North. Labour's hold of a marginal seat in a mid-term by-election is widely considered to have helped convince the Harold Wilson to call the 1966 election to seek a stronger majority. McNamara retained his seat at the 1966 general election, and at subsequent elections until the constituency was abolished for the February 1974 General Election, when he transferred to the new Hull Central constituency.

A Letter from The Minister

I later received correspondence from Fred Lee who had written to the Coal Board and the National Union of Mineworkers asking for their comments. I did not however receive a copy of their replies but I was satisfied that by that time everyone at the pit knew about what the mechanics branch at the Rising Sun had done. I let the matter of standing for parliament die a death, not even mentioning it locally to the branch. Quite a number of the mechanics were not Labour, especially the electricians, and it would not have gone down well at all. This all occurred in 1965, and a press statement in the local newspaper dated Friday 17th December said: "Councillor Ron Curran, secretary of the Wallsend branch of the Northumberland Colliery Mechanics' Association, and his fellow branch officials, have achieved their immediate objective. They have brought the issue of pit closures directly to the notice of the Prime Minister, Mr Harold Wilson. The branch is staging its battle against the threat to close the Rising Sun".

The Protests Against Closures Begin!

Right: *Wallsend Colliery Mechanics Committee in London on 17th February 1966 to lobby Parliament about colliery closures, seen in Trafalgar Square considering pigeon pie for their next meal. From left to right: First not known; George Wharrior, fitter; Ben Robinson, fitter; not known: Ron Curran, blacksmith; Ken Curran, fitter; Bob Coulson, electrician; John Farnell, electrician.*

About a dozen of our branch committee travelled to London with 25 officials and committee of the Wallsend Miners' Lodge to join a mass rally about pit closures and to lobby Parliament afterwards. After a coach journey I thought was never going to end we arrived. We proceeded to an underground station and one of the funniest scenes I have ever witnessed off the screen took place before our eyes. The banner carriers were told they had to go down a spiral staircase with their twelve foot poles. They went into a huddle to discuss how to do it safely and came up with the idea to send one person in front and another behind so that the poles would not injure anyone. The man at the front was a member of the welfare Jolly Boys who entertain the old folk at the Christmas Treat. As he started down the stairs he started yelling "Is there anybody there?" and a female voice replied faintly "Yes, who is it?". He replied, "It's me pet. I have a long pole and I wouldn't want it to damage you". There was a silence and then the patter of women's shoes going away into the distance. There was a number of individuals that we passed on the stairs without damage and when we got to the bottom a railway policeman was waiting with a young woman.

He looked in amazement at the two pole carriers and asked who had called a derogatory remark to this lady. They all pointed to each other with a big grin. Then the man responsible went up to him and said, "Well if it was you coming up the stairs you wouldn't want this pole in your eye would you?" The penny seemed to drop and the policeman grinned and waved us on. However, getting onto the train was a major obstacle. There was a long end and a short end to each carriage and depending where they stood on the platform it was either easy or very difficult especially if the train was full, and it was of course. There was mayhem with short tempered Cockney's outraged at the bantering Geordies down from the hills, bawling to each other where to put their poles. One shouted to the customers on the train, "Where do you expect us to put them?" to which there was a roar of laughter. Eventually we arrived at our destination and went to rendezvous at Speakers Corner, Hyde Park. Hundreds of miners were present from as far apart as Northumberland, Durham, Yorkshire, Wales and Scotland, and many hoisted aloft posters and banners that said, 'Stop the Pit Closures', 'Coal before Oil' and 'Where's the Plan for Coal'.

Miners' Lobby Like a Gala Day
The Evening Chronicle, 17th February 1966

"Leading the men from the north through London's busy streets en route to the Commons was a contingent of 40 from the Rising Sun Colliery, Wallsend. Before the march began, Councillor Ronald Curran, one of the Rising Sun's delegates said: "We feel in our area that the opportunities for alternative employment are not as existent as the Government seems to think. The number of pitmen over 50 unable to find a job is a big problem. Facilities for retraining in the area is also insufficient." Councillor Curran said that the Northumberland miners felt, along with other pitmen throughout the country affected by the closures, that they had been badly let down by the Government who had gone back on some of their election promises. The miners wanted the Government to re-examine the whole policy of pit closures and at Westminster it was hoped to put a case to the Northern Group of MPs for at least a slowing down of the closures. Tomorrow miners' delegates are due to attend a special national conference at Congress House and there is a possibility that colliery mechanics officials will get the chance of a promised interview with the Minister of Fuel and Power, Mr Fred Lee."

The Wilson Government and the Coal Industry

The election of a Labour Government under Harold Wilson in October 1964 was welcomed by miners. Whilst few believed that the new administration would transform society, there was an expectation that there would be some reversal in the fortunes of the coal industry. Wilson was seen as a supporter of coal; he had been one of the architects of coal nationalisation and had underlined the importance of promoting miners' welfare at the 1960 Party conference. Much of Wilson's pre-election rhetoric had centred on 'the white heat of technological revolution', a vision which he proposed to bring about through a policy of increased investment in new industries and the modernisation and rationalisation of older sectors of the economy. What was not immediately apparent was the potential threat which this posed to workers in heavy industry, traditionally Labour's staunchest supporters. As the consequences of this policy began to be felt at pit-level, activists began to accuse the Wilson government of betrayal.

The Cat out the Bag!

Lord Robens, NCB chairman from 1961 to 1971, observed that: "Between 1965-66 and 1968-69, we closed no fewer than 204 collieries. This rate of a pit closure almost every week for four years was achieved under a Labour government. In fact under Labour, perhaps because of Harold Wilson's enthusiasm for technological change, we shut pits at a faster rate than when the Conservatives were in office. Indeed, a Labour administration could tap miners' loyalty and gain acquiescence for policies which would otherwise have been opposed."

As Dan Canniff, an Executive Council member in the 1960s, recalled candidly: "We bent over backwards for the Labour government."

This is an astonishing admission. It confirms everything that I had believed for some time. Nothing short of a government change of policy could ever lead to the closure of 204 pits in only 5 years from 1965 to 1969. It would have taken inefficiency or unexpected problems on an enormous scale for it to be otherwise. While we had geological problems at the Rising Sun it stemmed from an obstinate insistence in carrying on with mechanised equipment that would not fit the purpose, at very great expense rather than seek an alternative. Even the amount of waste, if proved,

Lord Robens at the Miners' Picnic.

would have to be on a vast scale for this kind of run-down of pit closures. Strangely enough, the period above includes up to 1969, the year that the Rising Sun Colliery closed. And was there ever an enquiry? Not on your life. How could there be, it would have been pointless given that they (the Government) intended to use gas and oil in the place of coal. However, a more complete story emerges with a report compiled by the University of Glamorgan in July 2006. This puts the lid on speculation and opens the door to the ultimate question, was Harold Wilson hiding from the miners themselves, and the nation at large, that he was closing the door on coal as an asset and a useful fuel commodity? Was he so much sold on the white heat of the technological revolution that he was willing to allow coal to die a death of starvation by oil and gas? I will let you the reader judge.

Union Man Defends Pit Axe
Newcastle Journal 16th June 1969

The decision to close the Rising Sun Colliery was defended yesterday – by a union man. With 90 per cent of the men at the colliery on guaranteed high wages, the new national wages structure for the mining industry could not have been implemented unless they got rid of the pit, said the Rising Sun NUM Lodge Secretary, Councillor G. Eland.

At a presentation to retiring lodge officials, the last function of the lodge, he said it was the first colliery not to object to its closure, and he had no regrets at the lodge decision not to do so. As lodge officials they could see the closure coming before it did. "We have transferred even boys to the Midlands with guaranteed high wages for three years," he said. "Afterwards it is up to them, but we don't allow the Coal Board or the Government to cut their standard of living." When he had first started at the pit in 1939, however, it was the biggest non-union pit in the area. Over the years it has been realised that there were two sides to every question.

Councillor Eland, along with the lodge chairman Mr G. Sutherland, the treasurer Mr W. W. McConnell, and the compensation secretary, Mr G. Gilchrist, received wallets of notes from the lodge for services. The gifts were presented by 72 year old Mr George Young, secretary of the Wallsend Mineworkers Federation for 28 years until his retirement five years ago. Mr R. Tait, acting manager in charge of the pit salvage work, presented long-serving certificates to 62 men, aged 55 and over, who went into early retirement when the pit closed.

These pearls of wisdom are bewildering? No man could say what George Eland said and at the same time claim to be fighting to keep the pit open. He travelled to London with scores of men to lobby Fred Lee at the House of Commons. I wonder if any of the 55 year olds at the presentation asked George if his compensation would last the ten years up to receiving his old age pension. No wonder the Journal appears astonished by his claim! R.C.

Chapter 9
The Sun Sets For Good
My Branch says Goodbye!

While I was living in Cleveland, on Teesside where I had lived shortly before being promoted to Newcastle, I received a telephone call from Stan Edgar, a young fitter who I knew well who now informed me that he was the branch secretary of the Rising Sun colliery mechanics. Did I know that the pit was closing, he asked and I said yes, my brother Ian who was still working there had informed me. He then said they wanted me to be their guest of honour along with Doreen at a dinner marking the official folding up of the branch, which would be held at the Gosforth Park Hotel, at Newcastle. "Everybody will be there, the manager (a new one called Mr Hetherington who I had never met) and top pit officials and all the electrical and mechanics officials and our union members. You will have to make a speech" he ended. And so Doreen and I turned up to see a packed dining room full of people that I had worked with for many years, some of them for the whole twenty five years that I had been employed at the pit, and quite a number that I had crossed swords with on a number of occasions.

To say that I was a little nostalgic at this event is to say the least. I was sad at the closure of the pit, and even sadder to see the demise of my 'own' union branch, that I had nurtured as its secretary for seventeen years. I was told that since I left the pit to go to college in 1966, there had been three other secretaries in three years, Ben Robinson an underground fitter, Geordie Wharrior another fitter and finally Stan Edgar, yet another fitter. It perhaps reflects the uncertainties and unrest that prevailed, when people did not know where their future lay and were pondering all the problems that redundancy would bring.

Right: *The last visitors – The agent and manager Mr George Hetherington (left) with 21 year old Brenda Tippet, from Wallsend Town Clerk's office, and the Mayor and Mayoress of Wallsend, Councillor and Mrs J. W. Hall at the Rising Sun Pit.*

On a personal note, however, I took my invitation to this dinner to be a great vote of confidence in my representations of the interests of the members over all those years. And it give me a great impetus to follow the same principles and initiatives that I had pursued throughout that time and carry them into my new career. I like to believe that I succeeded.

Sadly, the closing of the Rising Sun Colliery, meant for many, despite the cushion of redundancy payments, hardship and worry, about whether their Tom, Dick or Harry would get another job, almost certainly not as well paid (although less dangerous) and only of short term comfort. Redundancy never was meant to live the rest of your life on, and never could. Unfortunately for some it seemed a bonanza! Now there would be plenty of time to ponder upon whether there should or should not have been a greater effort to have explored the possibilities of keeping the whole industry viable. I now knew what is was like for Mr Chips in "Goodbye, Mr Chips" of film fame.

Setting of the Rising Sun

The relevant closure dates in its different stages courtesy of Jim Lucas Ventilation Officer are:

The last day of production:	25th April 1969
The surface fan switched off:	17th July 1969
Last man riding cage after closure:	18th July 1969
The G Pit fan switched off:	6th August 1969
Fire at No. 3 shaft:	6th March 1970

Albert Evans – the last man to come up the shaft on the last day of production, 25th April 1969.

It was on this day that my elder brother Ian, who worked at the pit for 28 years as a surface worker, brought his dad's bagpipes to the pithead, and played a regimental Scottish lament, Flowers of the Forest, as he walked slowly up and down past a number of colliery officials including the manager. He said later that he was sure some of them were crying.

The last cage up at the Rising Sun Colliery, on 18th July 1969. The men are: H. Lucas, Ventilation Officer (front left), H. Shand, Onsetter (front right), J. Pears, Joiner (back left) and T. Grindon (back right).

The Collapse of A Dream

The No. 3 shaft before and after demolition in February 1974. So many hopes of a new super colliery goes up in smoke?

I can add to that epitaph – it was a deliberate policy that marked the end of an entire industry. Never once in my experience was it even hinted to the miners that coal would be made totally redundant to be replaced by gas and oil. We were hoodwinked on a bewildering scale, in order I suppose to keep the wheels turning in the interim period. Nothing else stands up to public examination. So the industry didn't die, it was murdered! And the process was begun by a Labour Government! After all, you will have read what Alf Robens said?

Left: *The Final Straw! The destruction of No. 3 shaft tower. It did not survive beyond six years of productive life.*

Rising Sun Country Park

The *Evening Chronicle* on 20th January 1972 reported that £400,000 was to be spent on a reclamation scheme on the Rising Sun Colliery site. The plan was to turn 250 acres of pit heap and derelict land into pasture, farmland, woods and nature reserve. Above is some of the work taking place.

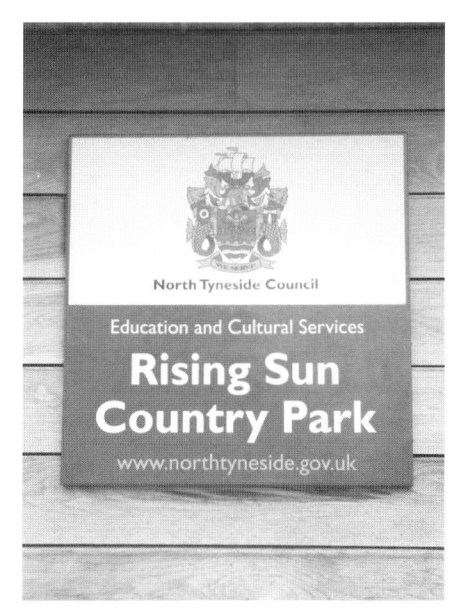

What is left is memories. A mole hill that was a pit heap (*above*). But we have in its place a nice Rising Sun Country Park.

Thanks For The Memories

The launch of the first edition of this book was very appropriately held at the Rising Sun Country Park, Wallsend, on the very date of the month 39 years after the colliery closed, Friday 25th April 2008. The pit closed on that day in 1969. The manager of the park, Mr Jerry Dronsfield said that he was very surprised at the number who had turned up and had he known, he would have made a larger room available. Nevertheless, we owe him our thanks for making available the very pleasant and accommodating room with a wonderful view looking towards the old pit heap.

Ron said: "It is below the ground where we now sit, that the Wallsend miners toiled and sometimes died."

Vincent Redhead, Les Francis, Ron Curran and Bruce Black seen together for the first time in 39 years.

The President of the National Union of Mineworkers, Ian Lavery, officially launches the book. On the left is Jerry Dronsfield, Rising Sun Country Park manager.

Doreen Curran with her brother, Grenville Stoneman and daughter Susan Wood.

This is a special photograph to me. It shows two of my former mates, both blacksmiths at the Rising Sun Colliery, Vincent Redhead (seated) and Bruce Black, in discussion with another former employee at the Rising Sun, Silvia Redhead wife of Vincent who worked as a secretary at the pit for many years. When she eventually left the NCB she worked as secretary at Ralph Gardner Secondary School in North Shields, my former school.

Thanking Ian Lavery for his address and giving a welcome to old comrades and their relations.

Introducing Ian Lavery to my wife Doreen.

Alex Allerdyce's two sons: Steve (left) and Dave (right) with Ron and Doreen Curran and Alex's sister-in-law Audrey Kay, sister of Sylvia Allerdyce deceased (née Kay).

Left to right: Peter Flannery (joiner), Alan Graham (electrician), Johnnie Farnell (electrician), Bob Clarke (fitter), not known, Bob Stonebank (electrician).

Relations of Sid Keddy junior. I knew Sid's parents well when they lived in Whitley Bay.

Deep in discussion – it's starting to look serious!

Let's all of us have a good read.

Also available from Summerhill Books

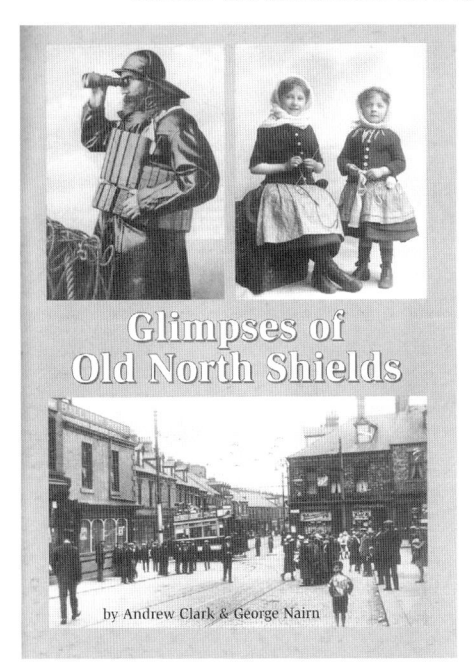

Glimpses of
Old North Shields

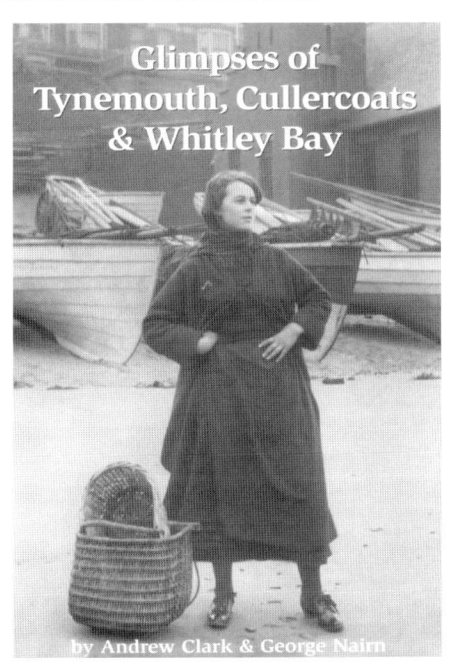

Glimpses of Tynemouth,
Cullercoats & Whitley Bay

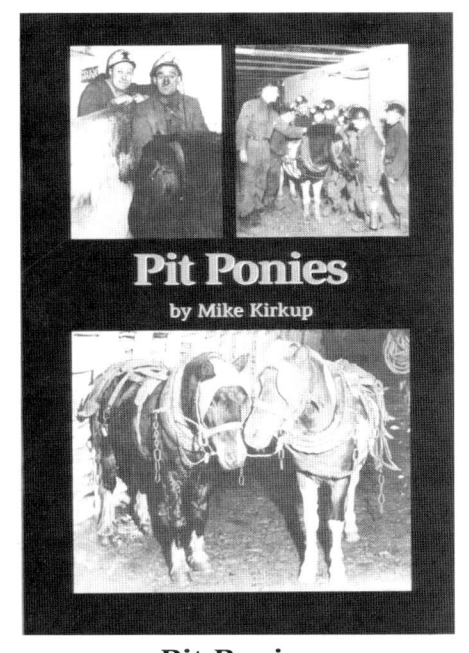

Pit Ponies

Banners of Pride